GREEK TYRANNY

The tyrants of Greece are some of the most colourful figures in antiquity, notorious for their luxury, excess and violence, and provoking heated debates among political thinkers.

In this well-contextualised study, Lewis examines the development of tyrannical government in theory and in practice, embracing lesser-known rulers such as the *tagoi* of Thessaly and the Hecatomnids of Halicarnassus, as well as canonical figures like the Pisistratid rulers of Athens and the Dionysii at Syracuse.

In the course of an assessment of the responses which tyranny evoked, Lewis replaces the long-standing theory of an 'age of tyranny' in Greece with powerful new arguments, suggesting tyranny was a positive choice for many states.

Sian Lewis is Lecturer in Ancient History at the University of St Andrews. Her books include *The Athenian Woman: an iconographic handbook* (2002; shortlisted for the Runciman Prize 2003) and the edited volume *Ancient Tyranny* (2006).

GREECE AND ROME LIVE

Also available in this series:

Forthcoming titles:

GREEK TYRANNY

Sian Lewis

BRISTOL
PHOENIX
PRESS

To Max, beloved and best cat

Cover image: Damocles, 1866 (oil on canvas) by Thomas Couture (1815–79), courtesy of Musée des Beaux-Arts, Caen, France/Giraudon/The Bridgman Art Library.

First published in 2009 by
Bristol Phoenix Press
an imprint of The Exeter Press
Reed Hall, Streatham Drive
Exeter, Devon EX4 4QR
UK
www.exeterpress.co.uk

British Library Cataloguing in Publication Data
A catalogue record for this book is available from the British Library

Paperback ISBN 978 1 904675 27 3
Hardback ISBN 978 1 904675 53 2

Typeset by Carnegie Book Production, Lancaster in Chaparral Pro 11pt on 15pt
Printed in Great Britain by Short Run Press Ltd, Exeter

Contents

ACKNOWLEDGEMENTS

I have been thinking about Greek tyranny for a long time; in 1986 my undergraduate tutor, George Cawkwell, suggested to me that I might like to write a study of the topic during the summer vacation. I found other things to do that summer, but although that first study was never written my interest in tyranny continued, in both teaching and research, and I would like to thank the many people who have helped me with the project over the years. First, I am grateful to John Betts at Bristol Phoenix Press for commissioning this book, and to Anna Henderson at Bristol Phoenix Press for her patience in waiting for it, and her editorial assistance. I would also like to thank the many students at Cardiff and St Andrews who have followed my courses on classical Greek tyranny and responded with enthusiastic and thought-provoking discussion, in particular William Rees, whose interest in the finer points of Agathoclean coinage was inspiring, and who gave me considerable assistance in the final stages of writing. I am very grateful to all the participants at the classical tyranny conference held in Cardiff in July 2003, especially Roger Brock and Slawomir Sprawski, for their contributions to the topic and for continued discussion. Roger Brock read the completed manuscript and made many very helpful comments and suggestions, while my Edinburgh colleague Lloyd Llewellyn-Jones stepped in with bibliographic assistance at a critical moment; Mike Bishop very kindly drew the map.

Finally I would like to thank my parents, Colin and Diana Lewis, for their unfailing support, and Robin MacKenzie, who lived with the writing of this book for a long time and without whose encouragement it would not have been finished. It is dedicated to our cat, Max, who kept me company at my desk as I wrote and who is sadly missed.

SL, September 2008

GLOSSARY

aisymnetes – a sole ruler appointed to arbitrate a civil dispute or crisis

archon – 'ruler', often used as the title of a chief magistrate

autonomia – independence, self-government

basileus – king (pl. *basilees*)

basilissa – queen

beltistoi – the 'best', the aristocracy

boule – council

diallaktes – mediator

diolkos – the stone trackway by which ships and cargo could be dragged across the Isthmus of Corinth

drachma – a unit of currency: in fourth-century Athens 1 drachma was a day's wage for a skilled labourer

dynasteia – power, rulership

dynastes – lord, ruler

epimeletes – overseer

gynaikonomoi – magistrates (literally 'controllers of women') who enforced laws relating to luxury and social display

hubris – violence or outrage against an individual

hoplite – heavily armed warrior

isonomia – equality before the law

kratistoi – the most powerful

mageiros – a butcher, also one who officiates at an animal sacrifice

monarchia – sole rulership

plousiôtatoi – the richest

polemarch – a magistrate elected to serve as leader in war

polis – city state (pl. *poleis*)

politeia – Aristotle's 'mixed constitution' between oligarchy and democracy

prytanis – a magistrate, often the cheif magistrate in a *polis*

satrap – regional governor within the Persian Empire

stasis – civil unrest

strategia – generalship

strategos – general

strategos autocrator – general with supreme authority

tagos – warlord, ruler of Thessalay (pl. *tagoi*)

tyrannos – tyrant

Map of the Greek World

Sinope

Heracleia

Byzantium

Chersonnese

onia

Thasos

Lampsacus

Cyzicus

Assos

Phrygia

Mysia

Pherae

Mytilene

Atarneus

rsalus

Lesbos

Lydia

Euboea

Chalcis

Sardis

otia

Eretria

hi

Thebes

Chios

Erythrae

egara

Samos

Magnesia

Athens

Myrus

Corinth

Caria

Pisidia

Epidauros

Miletus

Cilicia

Naxos

Mylasa

Halicarnassus

Cos

Lycia

Rhodes

©mcb

ABBREVIATIONS

CAH²	*Cambridge Ancient History*, second edition.
FGrH	F. Jacoby, *Die fragmente der griechischen Historiker*, (Leiden 1923-) [followed by author number and fragment number].
Fornara	C.W. Fornara, *Archaic Times to the End of the Peloponnesian War* [Translated Documents of Greece and Rome 1] (Cambridge 1983).
M-L	R. Meiggs and D. M. Lewis, *A Selection of Greek Historical Inscriptions to the End of the Fifth Century* BC (Oxford 1969).
Schwenk	C.J. Schwenk, *Athens in the Age of Alexander: the dated laws and decrees of 'the Lykourgan era' 338–322* BC (Chicago 1985).
R-O	P.J. Rhodes and R.G. Osborne, *Greek Historical Inscriptions 403–323* BC (Oxford 2003).

INTRODUCTION

Greek history is full of tyrants, from the shadowy Pheidon of Argos in the eighth century BC to the inventive Hieron II of Syracuse in the third, and they are some of the most colourful figures in classical antiquity. We hear of Artemisia II of Halicarnassus, the sister, wife and co-tyrant of Mausolus, who after her husband's death in 353 was attacked by the inhabitants of Rhodes, indignant that a woman should hold power over the cities of Caria. Artemisia captured their ships by a stratagem and killed the invading force; then she embarked her own army on the Rhodian ships, sailed to their city and used them to capture Rhodes itself for her empire. As a monument to her victory she set up a pair of huge bronze statues in the harbour, showing herself putting a brand on a woman representing the city of Rhodes (Vitruv. *De arch.* 2.8.14–15). We hear of the terrible death of Agathocles of Syracuse, killed with a poisoned feather in 289 BC: Menon of Segesta gave him the feather to pick his teeth after dinner, and Agathocles contracted gangrene in the mouth. Unable to cry out because of his disease, he was laid on his funeral pyre still conscious, and was burnt alive, a fitting punishment, according to the historian Diodorus, for the slaughter and cruelty of his reign (Diod. 21.16). And we find the cautionary tale of Polycrates, tyrant of Samos, who enjoyed enormous wealth and prosperity in the late 500s BC, but feared that the gods would bring him to disaster in jealousy of his good luck. He therefore decided to throw away his most valued possession, an emerald and

gold signet-ring, in the hope that this would avert the fate which
the gods had in store for him, and so dropped it into the open sea
from a galley. A few days later a fisherman caught an exceptionally
big fish and presented it to the tyrant, who received it gratefully;
but when the fish was cut open, Polycrates found his ring in its belly
and he realised that he could not stave off the fate which awaited
him (Hdt. 3.40–3).

Tyrants dominate Greek history, and their stories tell us much
about Greek attitudes towards rulership, but what exactly was a
tyrant? In modern times we use the term to describe the worst
kind of ruler – someone who exploits his or her power for personal
ends, irrespective of the law. Hitler and Stalin immediately spring to
mind, as do more contemporary examples in Central America, Africa
and the Far East. For the ancient Greeks, however, a tyrant was not
necessarily a bad leader: originally the word was used to describe a
situation where one man (or woman) who was not a monarch took
and held power within a state. In its original sense 'tyrannos' simply
carried with it the idea of absolute and personal power, distinct
from that of a king whose rule was bound by constitutional laws. A
Greek tyrant might choose to abide by the laws, and many did, but
the choice was his to make. Some of the many Greek tyrants whose
stories we know were the very worst of rulers, like Phalaris, the
tyrant of Acragas, who burned his enemies alive in a brazen bull, but
others, such as Pittacus at Mytilene, were remembered favourably
by their citizens as wise and moderate rulers or even sages, who
brought prosperity and peace to their cities. Later on in Greek
history the word came to have more of its modern flavour, implying
a ruler whose sole motivation was power and personal gain, and as
a result its use in public life became more controversial.

Tyranny and the *polis*

Why study tyranny when Greece is, after all, famous for originating democracy? Tyranny has often been treated by modern writers as a short and regrettable stage on the road to democratic government, a phase through which all Greek *poleis* had to pass, but which was left behind as the state matured. Nothing could be further from the truth of classical Greek government: relatively few states adopted democratic constitutions, and most Greek *poleis*, at most times, were governed as oligarchies by small groups of wealthy men. Democracy was treated with suspicion; only in Athens did it prove particularly successful and durable, and it is purely because of the Athenian dominance of our sources that democracy has gained so great a prominence in our conception of classical Greece. Although oligarchy was the most common political choice, tyranny also existed throughout the archaic and classical periods, and studying it therefore gives us an understanding of the political forms actually used in classical times.

As an example of the centrality of tyranny in Greek political life it is useful to consider the constitutional history of the city of Sicyon in the Peloponnese, a medium-sized mainland *polis* which was involved in, though rarely central to, major events between 750 and 200 BC. The early history of the state is related by Pausanias in his *Guide to Greece*, from its founding by its first king Aigialeus and subsequent renaming after the later king Sicyon. The Sicyonians then recorded a list of twenty-five kings, some native and some foreign invaders, taking the story through the heroic era down to the Trojan War, although there is no sign that these kings were more than myths. By the seventh century the city had developed a form of aristocratic rule, with annual magistrates; against this background we hear of the institution of a tyranny by Orthagoras, son of Andreas. The Orthagorid tyrants ruled for 100 years, and included the wealthy and renowned Cleisthenes, who held a year-long competition for his daughter Agariste's hand in marriage, attracting young princes from all over the Greek world and entertaining them sumptuously. Around 550 BC Aeschines (one of Cleisthenes' successors) was overthrown by the intervention of the Spartans and Orthagorid rule came to an end. We know little about the constitution which replaced it, but it appears to have been an oligarchy, which was made more restricted in 417. In the fourth century we hear of a new tyrant, Euphron, who seized power briefly with outside help and changed the constitution to a democracy; he was assassinated after a few years, and civil war between democrats and oligarchs followed. Demosthenes then tells us of two more tyrants in the 340s, Aristratos and Epichares, who were supported in power by the intervention of Philip of Macedon; after the battle of Chaeronea in 338, Sicyon, together with almost all the rest of Greece, came under Macedonian domination. We next hear of Sicyon in the period after Alexander the Great's death, when it was captured by Demetrius the Besieger during the Successors' Wars and rebuilt, once more with a democratic constitution. Pausanias then describes a series of no fewer than six tyrannies between 303 and 251, culminating in the famous Aratus, who restored 'equality of political rights' to the citizens and led Sicyon into the Achaean League, becoming its leader in 245 BC. The Achaean League was ultimately drawn into the war between Philip V and Rome in the 190s, and Sicyon fell under Roman rule in 146 BC.[1]

What can a history of this kind tell us? Sicyon experienced many different forms of government, with often rapid shifts from one constitution to another; it was under constant pressure, from inside and out, showed little political unanimity, and produced a constant stream of individuals looking to establish themselves in power. According to the Greeks themselves, political instability was a central feature of their states: Thucydides (1.18.1) comments on the unusually stable constitution of Sparta, which lasted for 400 years unchanged, as an exception to the norm, and Aristotle focused his political studies on the ways that one form of constitution changes into another. If such political flux was the normal condition for the Greek *polis* we may be wrong to expect to find stable and mature constitutions in any state. Certain features of Sicyonian history are typical of all Greek *poleis* – the tendency towards oligarchic rule as the norm, recurring factionalism between rich and poor, interventions by outside powers hoping to impose or encourage a government which will foster their aims, and the constant potential for the eruption of tyranny. There is a case for seeing the internal history of every Greek state as an unending struggle between would-be rulers and opponents of being ruled: aristocratic families saw political power as their hereditary right, states called upon charismatic leaders in time of war and then found them difficult to return to civilian status (a lesson also learnt in Rome), people found strong government attractive, placing their trust in men such as Pericles who effectively controlled public affairs, or groups within the state felt that their legitimate claims were being ignored, and looked to a champion against an unyielding government. Matters of day-to-day prosperity usually weighed more strongly than political abstractions, and so the time was always ripe for tyranny.

Secondly it is clear that Sicyon's two periods of greatest international presence and prosperity came under Cleisthenes and Aratus. Although few surviving authors have much good to say of tyrants, they were generally successful in government, bringing economic prosperity and expansion to their cities. Corinth under the Cypselids, Syracuse under Dionysius, Halicarnassus under Mausolus and Artemisia, all enjoyed their greatest international prestige and success under tyrannical rule; leaders such as Timoleon and Demetrius of Phaleron restored the fortunes of states which had been lost under more equal forms of rule.[2]

Greek thinkers did not necessarily oppose tyranny in all circumstances: it was often proposed that a sole ruler with overall control of military and political affairs was the best choice in times of danger. Demosthenes in the fourth century regretted the inefficient democracy in which he lived, thinking it incapable of offering the necessary organisation and leadership in war, and he contrasted the control over Macedonian affairs exercised by Philip as king: 'his having it in his sole power to publish or conceal his designs, his being at the same time general, sovereign, paymaster, and everywhere accompanying his army, is a great advantage for quick and timely operations in war ...' (Dem. *First Olynthiac* 4). Sicilian states elected a *strategos autocrator* (general with absolute power) in response to threat, in the same way that the Romans chose a dictator.[3]

There was always a tension between democracy and efficiency, between individual and state concerns, and a tendency towards autocracy at times of crisis – and crisis was a permanent state in classical times. Philosophers too saw tyranny of a certain kind as a positive thing; the radicalism of thinkers such as Plato is most clearly seen in this way, since although they lived and worked in democratic Athens, the philosophers of the fourth century constructed their designs for the ideal state around an enlightened monarch, the 'philosopher king', who could impose the best constitution on his subjects.[4] Instead of turning their collective back on tyranny in 510 with a shudder of relief, the citizens of Greece returned to this option time and again, seeing it as a solution to their problems or a means of bringing about necessary social change.

Sources for tyranny

Our sources for tyranny are very various. Although the Greeks gave us the concept of the tyrant, they did not invent the word for it themselves. *Tyrannos* came into the Greek language from the East in the seventh century, appearing first in the poetry of Archilochus and Anacreon to denote rulership with great wealth and power, like that of the legendary king Gyges of Lydia.

> I do not care for the golden wealth of Gyges, nor have I ever envied him, nor am I jealous of the great works of the gods, and I do not desire a great tyranny. All this is far off from my sight.
>
> (Archilochus fr. 19 (West))

It soon became a recognised term and the evidence of lyric poetry is often the best source for contemporary ideas about tyrants and tyranny because of its immediacy and personal voice. Aristocrats wrote about their own and their rivals' ambitions against a background of the social and economic changes in the seventh-century *polis*. When historians came to treat tyranny they recorded both realistic actions such as Artemisia's battle against the Rhodians, and folk-story tales like that of Polycrates and the fish. Some tyrants are described in entirely mundane terms, while others are surrounded by supernatural occurrences and oracles. The latter can be very revealing, because they show how rulers and subjects tried to create myths around tyrannical dynasties, often generating competing traditions. Dionysius I, for instance, attracted a whole set of stories illustrating his cruelty and paranoia, but himself offered accounts of oracles which predicted and supported his rule. Certain historians wrote histories full of praise or blame for individual rulers: Agathocles, by all accounts, was terribly traduced by the historian Timaeus, while Philistus, a relative of Dionysius I, wrote an entirely favourable account of all his actions. The debate about tyranny carried on well into Roman times, and we should always be aware of the context of a tyrant story – historians who describe tyrants are usually hoping to persuade their audience for or against the idea of tyranny, as we shall see. Inscriptions, too, can reveal much about individual tyrants – the titles they used, the way in which they were seen by their contemporaries, and their ambitions – and about broader historical developments: Athens, for instance, passed an intriguing series of laws against tyranny from the sixth century to the fourth.[5]

Tyranny was, as noted above, the topic of much philosophical debate, and we find discussions of its nature and efficacy in the works of Xenophon, Plato and Aristotle (as well as the Roman Cicero).[6] Aristotle in particular contributed to the analysis of tyranny as a constitution in his work on politics. The *Politics* is an extended discussion of the ideal form of constitution, and in pursuit of his theory Aristotle defines the various possible forms of government, explaining with examples how they come into being, are maintained, or fail. The work was based on the extensive research carried out into constitutions by Aristotle and his pupils at the Lycaeum: they travelled the Mediterranean collecting 158 constitutional histories from Greek and non-Greek states, and although only one of these constitutions now survives (the *Constitution of Athens*, discovered on papyrus in Egypt in 1890), the fragments detectable in the *Politics* and other works such as the *Oikonomikos* contain much of the solid evidence for the acts of tyrants.

Defining the tyrant

It is from Aristotle that the definition of tyranny most commonly quoted comes: 'When one man rules without legal restraint over his equals or betters, and rules entirely for his own benefit, not for that of has subjects, this must be the third [and most typical] kind of tyranny' (*Politics* 1295a 19–23). Aristotle cast tyranny in a very negative light, as a form of monarchy which has 'deviated' from the ideal, and by listing the characteristics of the tyrant – he rules over unwilling subjects, governs despotically, has a bodyguard of foreigners to protect him – makes it sound as though tyranny is a clearly defined constitutional form.[7] In practice, however, powerful autocratic rulers came in many forms: those who seized power by their own efforts, those appointed by a state to take control in a crisis, and those technically governing as representatives of a greater power, but in fact acting with complete autonomy. A brief survey of Greek tyrants demonstrates how hard it is to find a consistent definition of tyrannical power. If a tyrant is defined purely as someone who seizes power outside the constitution, then some of the most famous Greek exemplars certainly fit this pattern: Pisistratus, for instance, who took power in Athens on his third attempt in 560 with the aid of soldiers from Naxos and Argos, or Dionysius I, who used Syracuse's war with Carthage to establish himself as sole ruler. Pittacus of Mytilene, on the other hand, was an elected magistrate, not a usurper, and one of the very first tyrants and Pheidon of Argos, began, according to Aristotle, as a king. Others we would more naturally describe as governors: Demetrius of Phaleron, effectively tyrant over Athens from 311 to 301, was an agent of the Macedonians, and Mausolus and Artemisia in Halicarnassus were *satraps* for the Persian King.[8]

There are two reasons for the apparent haziness of our definitions. First, although Aristotle is very important to our understanding of ancient constitutions, we should remember that he was imposing a system of his own invention on Greek history, and one which did not always fit every case. He admitted that some kinds of monarchy were hard to place within his analysis – some tyrants are legitimately elected, and some kings wield tyrannical power. His long discussion of the survival of tyrannies in Book V includes both kings and typical tyrants without concern for technical accuracy. But it is also difficult to offer an acceptable definition of a tyrant because the Greeks themselves did not apply the term consistently. Before Aristotle the meanings attached to titles such as *basileus* (king), *tyrannos* and *dynastes* were imprecise, and there is often confusion in our sources about the appropriate title for a ruler. Even in the early period people were sensitive about the titles they used: a ruler might describe himself as a *basileus* while his subjects termed him *tyrannos*, and a man whose actual role was as *strategos* might be characterised as a tyrant by contemporary writers. As the term 'tyrant' became less acceptable in the course of the fifth century, rulers began to seek less controversial alternatives to describe their position: the Hecatomnid rulers of Halicarnassus, for instance, called themselves *dynastes*, while Dionysius of Syracuse referred to himself as *archon* of Sicily, a neutral term which simply meant 'ruler'. In the fourth century *tyrannos* tended to be applied much more widely as an all-purpose political insult, and we find rulers who are quite clearly not tyrants in the Aristotelian sense being so described by their contemporaries, from the 'Thirty Tyrants' at Athens to the oligarchic junta at Thebes in the 380s.

But even if there was no such thing as a constitutional position of 'tyrant', there were classical rulers who for a long or short period of time dominated a state and had the ability to do whatever they wanted – found cities, move populations, wage war, create new citizens, build monuments or accumulate money. We will therefore be considering a wide variety of rulers with certain fundamental features in common. They will be sole rulers, as individuals or as families, with direct and personal power over the state, unconstrained by political institutions. Their power will be dependent not on a right to rule, but on their own ability to command and retain power. Perhaps because of the insecurity of their position, tyrannical rulers also tend to have grand ambitions: they are empire-builders, colonisers, conquerors and constructors. Aristotle says rather cynically that tyrants' building projects such as temples and public fountains (and indeed the Egyptian pyramids) were intended to keep the people poor and prevent them plotting revolution (*Politics* 1313b 18–25), but in fact most tyrants presided over prosperous states. Other features which link tyrannical rulers are a concern for money, both in amassing and ostentatiously using a personal fortune and in generating wealth within their city, and the aim of establishing a hereditary rule. All tyrants aimed to hand power on within their family, and some succeeded in establishing a rule lasting many generations: Orthagoras at Sicyon, for instance, was followed by Myron I, Aristonymus, Myron II, Isodamos, Cleisthenes and Aeschines.[9] For this reason, far more tyrants inherited power than ever usurped it, making definitions still more problematic.

Tyranny and the Greeks

Greek attitudes towards tyranny, as already noted, changed over time, shaped by external events. In the beginning it figures in the poetic sources as an enviable thing, a status to which an aristocrat might aspire. The tyrants of the archaic age – Cypselus, Cleisthenes, Pisistratus and Polycrates – were popular, presiding as they did over an era of prosperity and expansion. But these attitudes shifted in the course of the fifth century, above all under the influence of the Persian invasions under Xerxes in 480/79 BC. Most of our sources for Greek history are Athenian, and the defining moment of the Athenian state was the establishment of the democracy in 510, and the amazing defeat of Persia in the next generation. The outcome of the Persian War was interpreted as the success of the free and democratic Greeks against the autocratic and tyrannous Persian King (faulty though this interpretation may be), and consequently in Athenian writing after 480, tyranny became the hated opposite of democracy. This coloured attitudes towards tyranny in the past as well; rulership which had previously seemed positive and acceptable was condemned as oppressive and self-serving. The Corinthian Sosicles says in Herodotus that 'there is nothing more unjust or bloodthirsty among men than tyranny'. (Hdt. 5.92a). After the Persian Wars, moreover, our sources shift their focus to Athens and its growing empire, and the question of tyranny (except in the abstract) becomes less urgent. This is not to say that there were no significant tyrannies in existence in the fifth century, just that it becomes harder to detect them. Even so, politicians in Athens constantly accused one another of wanting to establish a tyranny, and when the democracy was briefly overthrown in 404/3 by a group of thirty oligarchs, they gained the name 'Thirty Tyrants'.[10]

Tyranny reappears in fourth-century histories, partly reflecting a genuine change in political circumstances, as impoverishment after the Peloponnesian War and an increase in foreign interference meant that constitutions became very unstable, and partly because of a growing interest among philosophers in the consideration of political forms. Thinkers such as Aristotle and Plato led an intellectual movement in favour of enlightened ('philosophical') monarchy which opened up debates about the role of the ruler and the success of democratic and oligarchic regimes, and Xenophon presented figures from the past such as Cyrus the Great of Persia as 'ideal kings'. By the end of the fourth century Philip of Macedon had conquered the Greek states and put an end to their political freedom, and under Alexander the Great, a huge Macedonian empire was created. This too spawned new tyrannies and monarchies, at first under Macedonian rule as a form of government, and then, after Alexander's death, as independent kingdoms established by his successors and imitators. In some ways the process comes full circle at this point, as the third century saw the creation of new tyrannies which were less and less distinguishable from hereditary monarchies, such as the rule of Hieron II in Syracuse.

The very nature of tyranny produced some confusion of thought: however strongly one disapproved of a tyrant ruling free citizens, the idea of unlimited power and money remained very tempting. We should therefore not be surprised that attitudes towards tyrants can seem inconsistent. When tyranny first appears in archaic poetry, poets state that they (or rather their personae) don't desire or envy a tyranny, setting in train centuries of moralising which fails to hide the lure of the position. Writers dwell on the luxurious life enjoyed by the tyrant, the adulation (enforced or genuine), the access to women and boys, the food and drink and the opulently furnished palaces, while at the same time lamenting the corrosive effects of such indulgence on the character. Xenophon, in the fourth century, devoted a whole dialogue, the *Hieron*, to a demonstration that although the tyrant might appear to be the happiest and most fortunate of men, he is in fact completely miserable, friendless and paranoid: the wise man, he concludes, would avoid tyranny like the plague. Needless to say, when philosophers adopted the idea of the benevolent tyrant who would lead his city to enlightenment, they found it easy to identify potential candidates for the position.

Modern interpretations

In modern scholarship tyranny has gone in and out of fashion. Since Andrewes' 1956 study, *The Greek Tyrants*, the tyrannies of the seventh and sixth centuries have been a strong focus of study, with questions about the relation of early tyranny to kingship, and whether tyrants represent the growing power of the *demos* or of the army. Likewise the return to monarchic rule after Alexander has attracted much attention. More recently, partly in response to contemporary events and partly as a reaction to the concentration on democracy which peaked in the 1990s, a greater interest in fourth-century and Hellenistic history has arisen, and tyrants have been recognised as central here too; scholars are divided as to whether this should be seen as the resurgence of a successful political form or as a failure of democracy. Many books examine tyranny as a part of Greek political development and its role as a concept in Athens; fewer, however, consider tyrants throughout the classical period. Only very recently have studies appeared which question the representation of tyranny in historical sources, suggesting that our views of the phenomenon have been shaped by the constructions of individual authors.

What this book aims to do is examine tyranny from a positive perspective, for what it had to offer to both the individual *polis* and the wider world. We will look across the whole span of rulers, from Gelon in Syracuse, who commanded the largest army of his age, to Mausolus in Halicarnassus, who built for himself the greatest tomb in the known world. We will look at the *epimeletes* Demetrius of Phaleron at Athens, who was decreed 360 bronze statues by the *demos*, put up in less than a year, and the *tagos* Alexander of Pherae, who had to leave the theatre during a performance of Euripides' *Trojan Women*, because he was ashamed to be seen weeping at the misfortunes of Andromache on stage when he had killed so many of his countrymen without a qualm. We will look around the Greek world, putting ideological and philosophical concerns second to active politics and seeing what benefits a tyranny could confer, rather than taking negative characterisations at face value. We will address some fundamental questions: could a Greek state be successful only when the citizens were free, or did it need a single-minded ruler to lead the city to greatness? Why were some tyrants remembered both as bloodthirsty maniacs and as wise lawgivers? Should we see 480 as the high point when tyrants were eradicated from Greece, and the fourth century as a failure when they returned? Was tyranny good for those who experienced it or was it bad?

CHAPTER 1

ARCHAIC TYRANTS

A round 590 BC Cleisthenes, the tyrant of Sicyon, wanted to
find a husband for his daughter Agariste. Keen to make a
prestigious match, he announced at the Olympic Games that any
man who considered himself worthy to become Cleisthenes' son-in-
law should present himself in Sicyon within sixty days. Suitors came
from all over Greece – from Athens, Euboea and the Peloponnese,
from Aetolia and Thessaly in central Greece, from Molossia to the
north and from Sybaris and Siris in Italy – princes and sons of
noble houses. Cleisthenes kept the suitors at his court for a year,
testing their abilities and conduct in a specially built racetrack and
palaistra, in conversation and at lavish dinners. After a year, he
held an extra-grand dinner to announce the betrothal, at which the
Athenian Hippocleides, until then the favourite, famously 'danced
away his marriage' by his drunken cavorting. So Megacles of Athens
became the lucky bridegroom (what Agariste thought of this is not
recorded), and the others were sent home with a gift of a talent of
silver each (Hdt. 6.126–30).

In this story Cleisthenes of Sicyon is the archetypal archaic
tyrant. He is powerful, successful and admired: his reputation goes
beyond the bounds of his city, as aristocrats compete to gain an
alliance with him. His wealth is unmatched and his hospitality on
a scale to match the Homeric kings – there is an obvious echo of
the legendary Tyndareus and his competition to find a husband for
Helen of Troy. But what made Cleisthenes so powerful? Where did

his authority and reputation come from? This chapter will examine the first tyrants of Greece, in the years between 750 and 550, attempting to say who they were, why they came to power and what they achieved.

The origins of tyranny

Thucydides offers an outline of the early history of Greece at the start of his *Histories*: after the Trojan War ended, he says, there was a period of colonisation during which the Ionian coast was settled by Athenians, and Italy and Sicily by colonists from the Peloponnese. After this:

> As Greece became more powerful and the acquisition of wealth became more important than before, tyrannies were established in most of the *poleis* – previously there had been hereditary kingships with specified privileges – revenues increased, and the Greeks began to construct navies and to look towards the sea.
>
> (Thuc. 1.12)

The appearance of tyrannies has been called the first real 'event' in Greek history, and we have many stories about the rulers who came to power between 750 and 650, the best known of whom are Cypselus and his sons at Corinth, Orthagoras and his descendants at Sicyon, Pheidon at Argos and Pittacus at Mytilene. (Tyrant houses were usually known by the family name of the founding ancestor, as with the Cypselids at Corinth or the Pisistratids at Athens.) We also have references to Theagenes at Megara, and tyrants from the Peloponnese and central Greece who are now no more than names to us. It is indeed striking that so many tyrants followed one another into power, and that this form of government should have predominated in the archaic period. A theory of constitutional development has been built on the foundation of Thucydides' comment, arguing that Dark Age Greek communities were ruled by kings, but early on the monarchies were overthrown to make way for aristocratic governments, which were in turn replaced by tyrannies. After about a hundred years the tyrants were themselves ousted to make way for more popular and inclusive forms of government. Although this is not exactly what Thucydides says, it has proved a very persuasive model for modern scholars, explaining tyranny as part of a process of political evolution. But how effective is this theory in explaining the advent of figures like Cleisthenes?

Almost all Greek states preserved traditions about kings at the beginning of their history. In most cases these kings were imagined to be firmly in the heroic past – before the Trojan War – and their stories saw them interacting with gods and mythical heroes. Thus the Athenians had tales of legendary kings including Cecrops who was half man and half snake, Erichthonios the son of Hephaistos, born from the earth of Attica, and Theseus who battled the Minotaur and the Amazons, while at Thebes we find the tragic tale of the house of the Labdacids, Laius, Oedipus and his ill-fated sons. In most cases, however, the Greeks did not think that their kings had lasted into recorded history: they were held to have been replaced by aristocratic governments at or soon after the fall of Troy. Only three *poleis*, Athens, Argos and Corinth, preserved records of post-heroic kings, and these are simply lists of names, invented to fill a gap between the end of the heroic age and the beginning of magistral records. Thucydides' claim about the transition from hereditary monarchy to tyranny is thus unconvincing: it is not clear that any state ever really had a ruling king, with the possible exception of Argos.[11]

If the kings of history were an invention, what did exist before tyrants? The poetry of Homer can tell us something about Greek society in the eighth century, particularly the *Odyssey*, which depicts life in Ithaca after the Trojan War. What we find are social structures with a group of powerful men at the top, referred to as *basilees*, one of whom, like Odysseus, is pre-eminent. *Basilees* were heroic men who excelled in strength and courage and traced their ancestry and rights back to the gods, but they were not 'kings' in the sense of a single ruling house which handed on power down the generations. Odysseus was not a hereditary king; when he failed to return from Troy, there was no assumption that his son Telemachus would inherit his position. Instead Ithaca had a group of ruling aristocrats, any of whom could become ruler in Odysseus' place: wealth and fighting prowess were the obvious qualifications.[12] Homer's Ithaca also had an assembly of the people, by consent of which Odysseus (or whoever else) ruled. We can see outlines of similar systems in historical *poleis*: all the wealthy nobles at the top of society were *basilees*, and power over law, justice and war was concentrated in their hands. Annual magistracies existed for particular jobs like command in battle or religious roles, but these were not of great importance, and in general the group ruled as a unit, closed to outsiders. It was a system based on privilege of birth, as power was limited to this small wealthy group who tended to intermarry.

The story of the tyrant Cypselus at Corinth illustrates the political reality of the seventh-century *polis*, and raises some interesting questions. How Cypselus came to power in Corinth around 650 BC is told in two versions, one from the fifth century in Herodotus' *Histories* (about 200 years after the event), and one by the fourth-century Nicolaus of Damascus (about 300 years later). Herodotus' story is like a folk tale in style: Corinth at the time, he says, was ruled by a group of two hundred called the Bacchiads (descendants of Bacchios), who held the political offices and married only among themselves. One Bacchiad had a daughter named Labda who was lame, and because he could not find a suitable husband for her among his peers, he married her to an outsider, Eetion. Eetion, who was childless, consulted the Delphic oracle about his lack of children, and was given an oracle predicting that Labda's son would come to rule Corinth. The Bacchiads heard about this, and remembering a similar oracle which seemed to predict the same thing, they decided to murder Labda's baby as soon as it was born. Labda, however, had divined their plan, so she hid the baby in a beehive, and when the Bacchiads came, search as they might, they were unable to find him.[13] When Cypselus had grown up, prompted by a further oracle he made himself tyrant over Corinth, overthrowing the Bacchiads and driving many of them into exile. Nicolaus, in contrast, tells a much more mundane story: after the abortive murder attempt by the Bacchiads Cypselus grew up in exile, returning to Corinth as a young man. He entered public life and became popular with the citizens, in contrast to the violent and insolent rulers. He became *polemarch* (leader in war) and increased his popularity by his generous actions towards the *demos*; eventually he became a leader of the people, staged a coup and killed the *basileus* Patrocleides. The people appointed Cypselus as *basileus* in his place, and he exiled the Bacchiads and brought back the citizens whom they had exiled. Cypselus' rule was mild and lasted for thirty years.[14]

Neither story is without its problems from a historical point of view, but they agree on the background against which Cypselus took power: the rule of the Bacchiads. The 200 nobles formed a ruling aristocracy, defined by birth, drawing from their number the magistrates who ran the state: the two titles we hear in the histories are the *prytanis* (the leading magistrate) and the *polemarch*. But the terminology used to describe the change from the Bacchiads to the tyranny of Cypselus is confusing. According to Nicolaus, before Cypselus there was a Bacchiad king, Patrocleides, whom Cypselus killed and replaced as king; it was not until Cypselus' son Periander took over that the rule became a tyranny. Strabo, on the other hand, describes the Bacchiad group collectively as tyrants, and suggests that Cypselus was merely replacing one tyranny with another (*Geog.*

8.6.20). Herodotus' story too contains a criticism of Bacchiad rule, with the idea that Cypselus was restoring justice when he took power. The accounts lack the clarity of Thucydides' formulations and seem unable to agree on the scale of the change between Bacchiad and Cypselid rule. So was Cypselus' rule as tyrant really different in quality to that of the Bacchiads, or was he just a new version of the same old regime?

We can turn for an answer to the relatively well-documented tyranny of Pittacus at Mytilene on the island of Lesbos. Ionia was the home of the earliest Greek poets, who wrote in their lyrics about personal concerns, such as drinking, warfare, love or politics. The poet Alcaeus, who wrote at the beginning of the sixth century, was an aristocrat, and was closely involved in the political life of the city: his poetry, though fragmentary, gives us an idea of what tyranny looked like from the inside. Alcaeus describes Mytilenean politics in terms of rivalry and conflict within a small group of leading men: they were all wealthy nobles, like Homeric *basilees*, but in an atmosphere of intense competition, with individuals or groups vying to take overall control of the state. Alcaeus played a full part in the power struggles – initially a ruler called Melanchros (described as a tyrant by Diogenes Laertius) was in power, and the poet's brothers joined forces with Pittacus to oust him. Trouble then seems to have arisen between Alcaeus' faction and Pittacus: they originally made a compact to oppose a new tyrant, Myrsilos, but Pittacus betrayed the agreement, changed sides and came to rule alongside Myrsilos (fr. 70). When Alcaeus' plot was unsuccessful, he went into exile (frs. 129–130), and subsequently his verse celebrates the death of Myrsilos, inciting his peers to 'drink with all their might' when Myrsilos is dead (fr. 332), but his side could not prevent Pittacus taking power. Alcaeus describes how he has been set up as tyrant over the city:

This gutless and ill-starred city has set up low-born Pittacus as tyrant, all of them loud in his praise.

(fr. 348)

Obviously his is a one-sided view, and later sources remembered Pittacus quite favourably, as we shall see, but what is clear is that the competition involved only the nobles: there is no sign that Alcaeus or his rivals were supported by, or interested in, the *demos*.[15]

Pittacus and Cypselus are similar in kind – aristocratic insiders who found a way to rise above their peers and become pre-eminent – and neither is quite the novelty he initially appears to be. Pittacus exercised power as tyrant in 590; but he succeeded Myrsilos, who himself had succeeded Melanchros; and before these Aristotle knew about an aristocratic group at Mytilene called the Penthelids, who went around in gangs beating people and were put down by one Megacles (*Politics* 1311b 26–30). Cypselus overthrew the Bacchiad Patrocleides, and the Bacchiads in turn were said to have formerly seized power themselves. So it seems that the idea of kings overthrown by tyrants is too simple – tyrants grew out of the competitive social structure of aristocrats, as they struggled to become the first among equals.

The tyrant and the city

But if the archaic Greeks perceived no clear difference between a *basileus* and a tyrant, they would not have adopted the new word to describe Cypselus and Pittacus. So exactly what was a tyrant? Aristotle saw the fundamental difference between a king and a tyrant as one of law: a king held power by law, but a tyrant ruled unconstitutionally. One might wonder, however, whether Aristotle was correct in thinking that early states like Corinth or Sicyon had a constitution as such for a tyrant to rule outside. No Greek state (apart from Sparta, it is claimed) had a written constitution in 650, and the fragments of early law which are preserved suggest that constitutions were only in the process of being created at this stage. The earliest inscribed law that we have comes from Dreros in Crete, dating from between 650 and 600; it states:

> ... The *polis* has decided: when a man is Kosmos (chief magistrate), the same man shall not be Kosmos again for ten years. If he does become Kosmos [again], whatever judgements he gives, he himself shall owe double and be without rights for the rest of his life, and whatever his decisions as Kosmos, they shall be as nothing. The swearers [to this shall be] the Kosmos, the Damioi and the Twenty of the *polis*.
>
> (M-L 2 (= Fornara 11))

The citizens of Dreros are clearly trying to establish how justice was to be administered, who was eligible to be magistrate and how long posts could be held; a law like this does not suggest the existence of a full constitution. The Spartan constitution known as the 'Great Rhetra', traditionally supposed to date to the seventh century, similarly demonstrates the rudimentary state of political forms at this stage:

> Build a temple to Zeus Syllanios and Athena Syllania, and divide the people into tribes and obai, and establish a council of thirty together with the kings; then from time to time hold an assembly between Babyca and Cnacion, and there bring in and transact (public) business. But the *demos* shall have the deciding power.
>
> (Plut. *Lycurgus* 6)

Looking at our tyrants again, it is not easy to see in what way they were 'unconstitutional' compared with the leaders who preceded them. At Miletus, according to Aristotle, Thrasyboulus became tyrant around 610 from his position as *prytanis* or chief magistrate, and Pheidon of Argos is said to have been a hereditary king who became a tyrant. The most relevant case here is that of Pittacus, whom Aristotle says was appointed as *aisymnetes*, meaning something like 'peacemaker', to oppose the exiles led by Antimenides and Alcaeus. Aristotle presents the role as an example of 'elective tyranny', an absolute ruler elected by the *demos* for a particular purpose, while Dionysius of Halicarnassus saw the *aisymneteia* as a parallel to the Roman dictatorship, which was used to provide a leader in times of crisis, either external war or civil unrest. Strabo (writing in the first century AD) claims that Pittacus 'used his *monarchia* for the overthrow of the powerful factions and ... restored the city's autonomy'. Strabo's phrase about restoring *autonomia* is vague, but Pittacus, far from overturning a constitution, actually helped to create one: tradition has preserved a second image of Pittacus, as a lawgiver who introduced a lawcode, including the provision that crimes committed while drunk should carry a greater penalty than those committed by sober miscreants.[16]

Pittacus was not alone among tyrants in creating new laws and institutions for his city: Cypselus most probably reorganised the tribal structure of Corinth, and his son Periander certainly introduced a *boule* (council), and passed laws to limit expenditure and display among the rich. Cleisthenes at Sicyon also reorganised the tribal structure of the state, creating four new tribes, and Aristotle comments on the Orthagorid tyrants in general that they were slaves to the laws. In this respect tyrants contributed to the creation of constitutions, rather than undermining them: as the institution of the *aisymneteia* shows, it was sometimes necessary for one man to be given power to intervene in civil strife or to set up and enforce new laws, and in this way the distance between a tyrant and a lawgiver could be very small. When Solon was appointed lawgiver at Athens in 594, the position was understood by his contemporaries as offering a stepping-stone to tyranny, although Solon himself declined the opportunity: he says in his poetry that had anyone else received the same power,

> He would not have restrained the *demos*, nor would he have
>   stopped
> Before he had stirred up the milk and taken the cream.
>
> (Arist. *Ath. Pol.* 12.5)

To say that a tyrant is an unconstitutional ruler, then, does not do justice to the complexities of the period, but in that case, what can we say marked the difference between a tyrant and a king? One feature stands out: the tyrant's relationship with the people. Since Homeric times, the class hierarchy had been fixed, and the poor had no role to play in civic affairs. We are fortunate in having a testimony from the lower strata of the early *polis*, in the form of the *Works and Days* of Hesiod, who describes life in a village in Boiotia from a peasant's perspective. To speak of a 'city' at all in this period can be misleading, as most Greeks lived in villages and scraped a living by farming, and it is this life which Hesiod describes. He presents an existence defined by the struggle against poverty, horizons firmly bounded by family and neighbours. Hesiod's world has government and justice of a kind, but it is something very distant from the farmers – Hesiod speaks of travelling to the city to settle a dispute, and of the 'bribe-swallowing judges' who preside (*W&D* 27–39). Hesiod's advice is that the peasant should avoid the *basilees* at all costs: no one will find justice with these powerful and grasping men, so the wisest course of action is to accept one's lot and apply oneself to farming.[17]

The seventh century, however, brought about significant changes in social organisation. As populations grew and spread across the Mediterranean, possibilities opened up for the generation of wealth

in ways other than through farming, and hence for social mobility.
Individuals could become rich through trade, while the foundation
of new cities in the Black Sea, in the West and in North Africa gave
the poor the chance to gain land and status in a new *polis*. The
impact of these changes on the old social order is described by a
sixth-century Megarian poet, Theognis:

> ... a noble man does not scorn to marry the low-born daughter
> of a low-born father, as long as the latter gives him a lot of
> money, nor does a woman refuse to marry a rich and low-born
> man; she prefers a wealthy husband to a noble one.
>
> (ll. 185–8)

Theognis was a nobleman who disliked the new order: he laments
the way that 'lowborn' men can become wealthy and the noble
become poor, and sees the city 'stirred up' by rival aristocrats and
heading for civil war:

> Cyrnus, this city is pregnant and I fear that it will give birth to
> a man who will correct our wicked insolence. The citizens are
> still of sound mind, but our leaders have changed and will fall
> into great evil-doing.
>
> (ll. 39–42)

Tyrannies arose at the same time as these developments, and
there has been a long-standing debate as to whether the tyrants
were leaders of a new movement for popular power, or products of
it. One school of thought proposes that the tyrants were carried to
power as leaders of a democratic uprising; a story of the humble
origins of Orthagoras, founder of the Sicyonian tyranny, is used
to lend support to the theory (Diod. 8.24). Aristotle also recounts
that Theagenes became tyrant of Megara in the second half of the
seventh century because he found the rich men's cattle put out to
graze on the commoners' land and slaughtered them (*Pol.* 1305a

24–6). This has been interpreted as evidence that Theagenes led an uprising against the aristocracy, although it is not explicitly stated in the story. Others associate changes in the style of warfare with the coming of tyranny: hitherto, only the aristocrats had taken part in warfare, with the people forming a crowd whose role was limited, but the evolution of the heavy-armed warrior (*hoplite*) led to the adoption of massed fighting tactics: hundreds of men standing shoulder to shoulder, forming an unbreakable unit. Once the citizens saw themselves as investors in their *polis*, fighting to protect their country, they tried to wrest political power from the hands of the aristocratic class, and tyrants were carried to power as representatives of the army. Pheidon has always been considered the classic example of this, with the idea that Argive success at the battle of Hysiai against Sparta in 669 marks the beginning of *hoplite* tactics, and that Pheidon was carried to success through *hoplite* support. In recent years, however, scholars have moved away from both these ideas in their extreme form, as the evidence for tyrannies which we have already looked at does not seem to indicate any such direct intervention in politics by the *demos*. In all the cases which we have seen, tyrants emerged from aristocratic groups fighting among themselves for power: there is no sign in the seventh or sixth centuries of a tyrant heading a popular party. Even the supposedly humble Orthagoras on closer inspection turns out to have held the sacred role of *mageiros*, presiding at sacrifices, and thus to have belonged to the aristocratic class. The protests of writers like Theognis suggest that there may indeed have been newly wealthy non-nobles attempting to join the ruling group, but such men simply wanted to become aristocrats, not to overthrow them. Similarly *hoplite* warfare, while it involved more men that traditional modes of fighting, nevertheless required soldiers to equip themselves with heavy bronze armour – hardly something which would allow more than a limited wealthy class to participate.

So the *hoplites* cannot be equated with the *demos* lending their support against the aristocracy.[18]

But even if tyrants were not democratic leaders, they did offer something new to the *demos*. Many of our descriptions of tyrannies focus on the idea of a ruler who will bring justice – Cypselus' oracle predicted this, and Theognis talks of a ruler who will 'set straight' the nobility's behaviour. Tyrants certainly positioned themselves as opponents of the unjust aristocrats, and gained the support of the people by actions such as exiling their rivals in the name of justice (which is probably the focus of the Theagenes story). More directly a successful tyrant like Pittacus could bring an end to factional fighting and civil war, allowing a city to prosper without internal strife. A tyrant was also in a position, as we have seen, to create or reform a constitution, and this too tended to work in favour of the *demos*, as public roles were regularised and laws established for all, instead of justice remaining in the hands of the nobles. Most significantly the relationship between tyrant and people had to be much closer than that of traditional aristocrats; a tyrant whose position was by its nature precarious had to be responsive to public opinion, and aware of the wishes of the *demos* as a group.

The achievements of tyranny

Definitions are well and good, but what did a tyrant actually do once in power? If the example of Cleisthenes of Sicyon is representative, a tyrant acted in much the same way as a king. He (and at this period they tended to be men, although we will meet Artemisia I in the next chapter) often lived on the Acropolis, the spiritual centre of the city, and while the idea of a bodyguard may be anachronistic, usually had some kind of armed group at his command. He did not carry out all the functions of the state himself – most tyrants allowed normal political activities to continue – but retained overall control of legal affairs, military matters and political appointments. He also, if our stories are any guide, lived a life of luxury and self-indulgence.

Most ancient sources make a close connection between tyranny and wealth. Both Archilochus and Anacreon refer to tyrants and wealth in the same breath (see p. 7 above), while Solon speaks of a man who might 'gain power and unbounded wealth, and become tyrant of Athens for only a single day' (Plut. *Solon* 14.6). Thucydides makes the connection explicit, saying that the importance of acquiring money was one of the factors contributing to tyranny, and that as a result of the tyrannies, revenues increased (Thuc. 1.18) and even Aristotle says that the aim of tyranny was to gain wealth, which facilitated a tyrannical lifestyle (*Pol.* 1311a 9–11). Certainly Cleisthenes was extraordinarily wealthy, and keen to demonstrate the fact, and at the root of this is a difference in approach to personal wealth and civic finance. The *basilees* of Homeric times were rich men because wealth was one of the factors which conferred status, and their wealth was personal, either inherited or gained through warfare and travel. Odysseus has his house, slaves, land and flocks and owns a large number of precious objects handed down by his ancestors or gifted by his hosts; in social terms his role is to provide for those lower down the scale, not to gain wealth from them. The tyrants who rose to power, on the other hand, gained their great wealth as part of the tyranny, enabling them to enjoy luxury and self-indulgence on a hitherto unseen scale. This is not to say that they were necessarily poor before becoming tyrants, but that becoming tyrant meant taking over the means to amass vast amounts of money. Along with the growth of the *polis* had come new methods of generating money in the form of taxes, whether on trade (import and exports, dues, harbour fees) or personal taxation (tithes of produce). Many tyrants were able, as sole leaders of the state, to oversee economic development: under Periander at Corinth the *diolkos*, the trackway for taking goods across the Isthmus, was constructed, and charges were levied, while Polycrates at Samos oversaw the creation of a market quarter in the city. They also took measures to control taxation – Periander is said by Strabo to have contented himself with the taxes from the harbours and agora, perhaps implying that Cypselus had levied more taxes. It is no coincidence that coinage first comes into use in the period around 600 BC, primarily to facilitate payments made by and to the state, such as the collection of fines and taxes and the payment of wages for soldiers and expenses for building projects.[19]

This might make us assume that tyrants were grasping and self-interested, and thus necessarily unpopular with their citizens, but this is far from the case. Assumptions about the unpopularity of a tyrant are often anachronistic – we have seen that concerns about political freedom have little relevance to the early period: a fourth-century Greek might resent his loss of political rights under a tyranny, but the *demos* of the early state had no political rights to lose, as Hesiod's poetry makes clear. Citizens of the early state judged their rulers on other criteria, and tyrants would not have lasted in power had they not been successful. We can trace several key areas where a community could benefit. The first is defence: in the warlike milieu of archaic Greece where small states constantly warred with their neighbours, having an accomplished general to lead the state could seem wise. Leadership in war and tyranny are intertwined throughout Greek history, and several archaic tyrants are said to have come to power after a successful campaign: Pheidon, as noted above, led the Argives to victory over the Spartans at Hysiai and also conquered the Eleians and took over the Olympic Games; Cleisthenes led the Sicyonians in their Sacred War against Argos; and Cypselos, if we believe the account of Nicolaus of Damascus, held the post of *polemarch* before gaining his tyranny. Pisistratus too is supposed to have made his name as a successful general in Athens' war against Megara. As well as protecting the state, or leading it in conquest, tyrants were also in a position to pursue long-term economic and civic goals. Under the Cypselids, for instance, Corinthian trade was assisted by the foundation of colonies along the west coast of Greece at Leucas, Ambracia and Anactorium, protecting shipping routes; Cypselus sent his sons to found these places and establish new tyrannies there, and his heir Periander did the same at Potidaea in the north. Control of manpower and finances allowed tyrants to institute large-scale building projects: Cypselus fortified Corinth, and Periander constructed the artificial harbour at Lechaeum, and Polycrates likewise created a harbour and markets at Samos. Under the Pisistratids a network of roads was constructed in Attica, unifying the territory with its civic centre. As well as projects of practical value, tyrants built to make their cities impressive: all constructed temples to beautify and protect the community. Cypselus built temples to Apollo in Corinth and Poseidon at Isthmia, and Periander the temple of Olympian Zeus, the largest in the Peloponnese. Cleisthenes built a temple in Sicyon, as well as the racetrack and palaistra for his competition, a stoa in the agora, and buildings at Delphi after his success in the Sacred War. The tyrants' aim was to put their city onto the grand stage, and to give a sense of identity and coherence to the citizens. Of course the individual tyrant also gained personal fame from such projects and enhanced his standing within the city, but he also benefited from the prestige of the city as a whole; the tyrant's power, which allowed him to organise and carry through long-term projects, was a major factor in the status gained by cities such as Corinth and Samos.[20]

The reason that these men were so keen to compete in large-scale building and dedication was that they were able to take a wider view, beyond their immediate state. One of the striking features of tyranny at all periods is the way that rulers in different cities co-operated and assisted one another. The aristocratic classes across the Mediterranean had always transcended local loyalties through travel and establishing friendships, and by meeting at religious centres like the sanctuaries of Olympia and Delphi to compete and forge connections. The tyrants, though, took international contact one step further by cooperating rather than competing. As each was pre-eminent in his own state, there was more to be gained from friendship and alliance than from competition. So we find intermarriage between tyrant houses, creating webs of obligation between fathers- and sons-in-law, and creating grandchildren who would have ties to both houses: Periander married the daughter of Procles, tyrant of Epidauros, Agariste numbered among her suitors Leocedes, son of Pheidon of Argos, Cypselus' daughter married into the family of the Philaids at Athens, and we hear that Cleisthenes initially favoured the Athenian Hippocleides as son-in-law, because of his ancestral link with the Cypselids. We also see tyrants offering practical help and advice in the gaining and maintenance of power: assisting each other into power, and therefore assuring themselves of support in the future, and supporting and advising each other (Thrasyboulus of Miletus famously advised Periander to cut off the 'tall poppies', men who stood out from the masses and might pose a threat to his position).[21] There are cases in which one tyrant is seen to foster another in neighbouring states, either to enhance his own security or to extend the influence of his state in foreign policy. Because of these links, some scholars have speculated that tyranny can be understood as a fashion, which spread from one city to another by peer interaction.[22]

Stories about tyrants

The analysis in this chapter so far has focused very much on practicalities, but this was not how later Greeks remembered the early rulers. The stories of Cleisthenes and Cypselus are a good indication of the type of traditions preserved about early tyrants: there is little practical detail on how they reigned, or under what regulations, and a great many entertaining stories to show how they came to power, and the impressive or wicked things which they did. It is usually quite difficult to tell whether a tyrant was a good or a bad ruler, as the traditions became so confused: Herodotus' account of Cypselus tells of oracles and a miraculous rescue which are favourable to the tyrant, and yet says that there is nothing more unjust or violent than tyranny. Nicolaus says that he was a wise and popular ruler (though still without much hard evidence), although Aristotle describes him as oppressive towards his citizens. In a similar way the Orthagorid tyrants at Sicyon were described by Aristotle as moderate and respectful of the laws, but according to Nicolaus, Cleisthenes was 'very violent and cruel'.[23] There are two reasons why ancient opinions are so divided: because it was all so long ago – a tyranny was often the first post-mythological event in a *polis'* history, and in an era before written documentation – and because since there was little actual evidence for an early ruler like Cypselus, ancient authors were able to shape the story according to their preconceptions, emphasising the side of tyranny which they wished. So Herodotus presents us with Periander the monster, who killed his wife Melissa and committed necrophilia with her body, who sent 300 boys from Corcyra to Sardis to be castrated and made into eunuchs, and who summoned all the women of Corinth to a festival in his dead wife's honour, then stripped them of their fine clothes and burned the garments as an offering (Hdt. 5.93, 3.48). Yet Periander was also remembered as one of the Seven Sages of Greece – Herodotus seems to preserve some of the wise maxims attributed to him in Book 3 – and was appointed as arbitrator in an international dispute between Athens and Mytilene.[24] The two aspects of his reputation simply co-exist in our sources.

The amount of supernatural material in the stories also served a purpose: the idea of the tyrant foretold by an oracle is extremely frequent in Greek history, and one which was to last into later times. Cypselos of Corinth has perhaps the most lively account of oracular foretellings, but similar tales were told about Pisistratus of Athens and Orthagoras at Sicyon. Cleisthenes may have inherited his power, but his ancestor Orthagoras, the first tyrant, received divine notification of his destiny: when his father, Andreas, accompanied a group of Sicyonian nobles to Delphi, the group received an oracle that whoever heard first that a son had been born to him when he returned home would become tyrant (Diod. 8.24). Similarly Hippocrates, father of Pisistratus, was sacrificing at the festival at Olympia, when the cauldrons of meat and water which he had prepared boiled over, even though he had not yet lit the fire. Chilon, the famously wise Spartan, happened to be passing and interpreted the omen to mean that Hippocrates should avoid having children, or if he had a son already, should disown him (Hdt. 1.59). What is the purpose of stories like this? First, to account for the unlikely success of the individual – he was marked out from before his birth for the position which he achieved. Second, to emphasise the separation of the tyrant from his fellow citizens – he is different, whether in a good sense or a bad.[25] Third, it answers a difficult question posed in later times: why did our ancestors not reject tyrannical rule? How could they have been so spineless as to tolerate a tyranny for a hundred years, instead of rising up to fight for their rights? This is a question which undoubtedly had more meaning in 400 BC than it did in 650 BC – the idea of the people having rights for which to fight was quite novel in the seventh century – but which was nevertheless embarrassing, and the oracle offered a clear answer: it was fated that the tyrant and his sons should rule, the gods had decreed it, and the people could not have resisted even if they had tried. As time went by tyrants became major figures in a state's history, often remembered for periods of prosperity, expansion and construction of religious or public buildings, so it was difficult to belittle their achievements from a political perspective: oracular approval helped to accommodate the tyrant as part of popular history.

These stories emphasise the variety and complexity of our traditions about the archaic tyrants, traditions which had often had hundreds of years in which to accumulate and be reworked. Simple definitions of tyranny and neat theories of political development are hard to uphold in the face of this evidence, as tyrants are said to both create and overturn constitutions, to champion and oppress the *demos*, and to harm and help the *polis*. It is clear, though, that the tyrants flourished in an era of growth and prosperity, and that they took advantage of this prosperity to make a significant impression on the physical appearance and constitutional development of their cities, and later traditions cannot successfully hide popular enthusiasm for tyrannical rulers. The Greeks remembered men such as Cleisthenes, Cypselus and Pittacus as larger-than-life figures, and we will see in the next chapter how events in the fifth century shaped the historians' attitudes towards them.

CHAPTER 2

THE END OF TYRANNY?

We come in 560 to the tyrant who has attracted by far the most study and discussion among modern historians, Pisistratus of Athens. Pisistratus was an energetic and interesting man – he attained power in Athens on one occasion by dressing up a tall young woman as the goddess Athena, and riding into the city alongside her in a chariot – who remained in power for forty years, and was succeeded by his sons, Hippias and Hipparchus. The most revealing part of the Pisistratid story, however, is the distortion which came to surround the end of the dynasty. Herodotus says that Pisistratus' sons ruled jointly until Hipparchus was murdered in 514 by two citizens, Harmodius and Aristogeiton. As a result Hippias became harsh and unpopular in his rule, and the Alcmaeonids, one of the leading Athenian families, first gathered a group of exiles and tried unsuccessfully to overthrow Hippias, and then when they failed, brought the Spartans in to oust him, which they duly did. By the end of the fifth century, however, Thucydides was moved to make a special study of the fall of the tyranny, because people had got it so wrong: they believed that the tyrannicides had killed Hippias, when in fact the victim was Hipparchus, and that the tyranny was brought to an end by their act, whereas it had continued for another four years. Thucydides hammered home once again the involvement of Sparta, but why should he have needed to make such an issue of it? [26]

If we look at popular, non-intellectual accounts of the end of

the tyranny we can see that the people of Athens were telling
a very different story. A statue of the tyrannicides Harmodius
and Aristogeiton was set up in the Agora, and was depicted on
pottery and coins. Songs celebrated their exploits, giving them sole
responsibility for ending Pisistratid rule:

> I shall bear my sword in a myrtle bough / like Harmodius and
> Aristogeiton / when they killed the tyrant / and made Athens a
> place of isonomia [equality].
>
> (Athenaeus Deipn. 695a–b)

In Aristophanes' comedies old men recall the glory days when they
fought against the tyranny and defeated it. Never mind that the
battle at Leipsydrion was a defeat for the democratic forces: seventy
years had turned it into a victory, the demos' finest hour. Gone, too,
was any positive memory about Pisistratus and his sons. Aristotle, a
non-Athenian and an outsider, preserves strong evidence for a mild
and beneficial rule by the Pisistratids – Pisistratus, he says, ruled in
a mild and humane manner, obeying the laws and keeping the peace,
while Hippias, before his brother's murder, was sensible and public-
spirited (Ath. Pol. 16.1, 18.1). In the popular imagination, though,
Pisistratus, Hippias and Hipparchus were suspicious, greedy and
cruel, quick to execute and punish. No one would want such a ruler,
and the city was better off without them.[27]

   In the seventy years between the end of the tyranny and the
writing of Thucydides and Aristophanes there had taken place a
decisive shift in political outlook which permeated not only public
opinion, but historical writings too, often at a fundamental level.
The cause of this was the Persian invasions, under the influence of
which the Greek attitude towards tyranny, and towards their own
past, underwent radical change.

The influence of Herodotus

The historian who documented this period was Herodotus, and it is from his *Histories* that much of our detailed information about the archaic tyrannies comes. As we have seen, he had much to say about Cypselus and Cleisthenes, and also about the last two tyrannies of the archaic era, those of the Pisistratids at Athens and of Polycrates at Samos. The accounts he gives, though, are cast in a particular form. Pisistratus' story, because of Herodotus' chosen narrative structure, is told in a series of episodes. The first dwells on the omens which foretold Pisistratus' rise to power, and the intrigues in which he engaged to achieve it. Pisistratus first tricked the Athenians into giving him a bodyguard, and used it to capture the Acropolis, but not long after this his enemies joined forces against him and drove him out. He then allied himself with one of them, Megacles of the Alcmaeonid family, and regained power with his support, through the ruse of the woman dressed as Athena who accompanied him in his chariot as he entered the city (Hdt. 1.59–60). We can see that Pisistratus was clearly in the same mould as Pittacus, intriguing with aristocratic groups within the city in a bid to become leader. His alliance with Megacles similarly foundered shortly after, and Pisistratus was once more forced to withdraw. This time he gathered an army with the help of his sons and allies abroad, marched on Athens and installed himself as tyrant. Herodotus sketches how Pisistratus consolidated his position – hiring guards, raising revenues and exiling his enemies – but goes no further in describing his methods of government (1.61–4).[28] He does not resume the story of the tyranny until Book 5, where he relates how Hippias and Hipparchus were overthrown (55–65). He refers briefly to Athens under the tyranny on a few occasions, while relating other events, but essentially reduces the tyranny to two episodes, rise and fall. There is much that he omits, as we can see from a comparison with Aristotle's *Constitution of the Athenians*. Pisistratus ruled in accordance with the laws, but placed himself at the head of the system of government: the appointment of annual *archons* continued, although we can see that Pisistratus had overall control of the process. Pisistratus' position as autocrat allowed him to make many reforms to benefit the citizens and improve the city as a whole. Aristotle says that he supported agriculture, giving grants of money to poor farmers so that they could retain their land, and thus gained in increased taxation on agricultural production. He also instituted travelling judges to resolve disputes within villages, so that men did not have to come to the city for justice, and indeed travelled about the countryside himself to 'inspect and reconcile disputants' (*Ath. Pol.* 16–17). We can compare the benefits of this system with the complaints of the peasant farmer in Hesiod's *Works and Days*: instead of the law being in the hands of distant and capricious nobles, it is dispensed by civil appointees on the spot. Pisistratus used some of the revenues for large-scale civic building projects, such as the Enneakrounos (Nine-Stream) fountain which brought a public water-supply to Athens, and the temple of Apollo. Like all tyrants, he was concerned to secure the transmission of power, and he gradually brought his sons and grandsons into public roles: Hippias held the *archonship* in 526/5 and a second Pisistratus, the tyrant's grandson, in 522/1. His sons continued the programme of civic improvements; Hippias created a network of roads linking all areas of Attica to the city, each road supplied with milestones giving the distance to the centre of Athens (at the altar of the Twelve Gods in the Agora) and an improving maxim, such as 'do not deceive a friend'. As well as uniting the territory of Attica in practical ways, the tyrants also enlarged the festival of the Panathenaia, in order to celebrate Athens on the international stage. Processions and sacrifices were held, and competitions in athletics and music, including a contest for rhapsodes, singers who recited epic poetry.

Tradition holds that through these poetic contests Hippias was able to gather together and write down the Homeric poems for the first time, collecting and comparing the different episodes told by poets, and building them into a coherent whole. If true, the compiling of the *Iliad* and *Odyssey* is probably the greatest debt which the world owes to the Pisistratids.[29]

The Pisistratid tyrants clearly had a great influence on the development of Athens, both on its physical fabric and its identity as a *polis*. Later tradition asserted that Athens grew strong under the democracy (and Herodotus states this explicitly, for reasons we shall see), but in fact the foundations of Athenian strength and ambition were laid under the tyranny. Why, then, when there was so much evidence for the benefits of the Pisistratids to Athens, was Herodotus so selective in his presentation and grudging in his praise? We can see the same process at work in his treatment of Pisistratus' contemporaries, Polycrates and Periander.

Polycrates we have already encountered as another great builder: Herodotus makes a point of describing the three remarkable feats of engineering to be seen at Samos, all achieved under the tyranny: the tunnel, the harbour and the temple of Hera. The tunnel, constructed by the engineer Eupalinos, was nearly a mile long, and was bored through a hill to bring water into the city. The harbour was built with a quarter-mile breakwater, and the temple of Hera was the largest of all Greek temples of its day (Hdt. 3.60). But despite this Herodotus' presentation of Polycrates is a good example of how a historian can influence our perception. We hear that Polycrates had seized power and initially shared it with his two brothers, Pantagnotos and Syloson; afterwards he killed the former and exiled the latter. After a successful reign of thirteen years, during which he made Samos into a formidable power at sea, Polycrates incurred the enmity of the Persian governor of Sardis, Oroites, and was lured by him to the mainland on the promise of great wealth to assist in his imperialistic ambitions (we can note the theme of wealth once again). As soon as he arrived Oroites had Polycrates murdered and his body hung up on a cross (Hdt. 3.39, 120–125). Herodotus' Polycrates exists as a one-act drama: the impression given is that the tyranny begins and ends with him: as his ambition becomes too great, he overreaches himself and is punished. The moral is reinforced by the story of the ring and the fish, which demonstrates that however great his success, Polycrates could not avoid the downfall which followed. The episode seems to make a point about inadvisability of becoming tyrant, but only because Polycrates' rule is presented in isolation. Other sources imply that he was part of a long-standing tyrant dynasty: his father Aeaces ruled before him, as well as a previous Syloson, most probably Polycrates' uncle; the family was clearly accustomed to holding power, and Polycrates' misfortunes did not spell the end of their rule. Syloson was restored as tyrant shortly after his brother's death, and his son, Aeaces II, ruled in the early fifth century. Herodotus does not exactly hide these facts, but shapes his account of the Samian tyranny to suggest that it was much less successful than it actually was.[30]

A final example of Herodotus' tendentious presentation of tyrants can be seen in the story of the end of the Corinthian tyranny under Periander. Its placement in the *Histories* is an oddity, because the fall of the tyranny is related in Book 3, before we hear the story of Cypselus and how he became ruler. As an explanation for the enmity between Corinth and Corcyra, we are told that Periander had murdered his wife Melissa, and that the younger of his two sons, Lycophron, discovered the truth from his grandfather Procles, the tyrant of Epidaurus. Father and son quarrelled, and Periander cast his son out of his house, ultimately sending him to Corcyra, which was under Corinthian control. When Periander was an old man, however, he decided to be reconciled with Lycophron and to make him his heir, so he agreed to move to Corcyra himself if Lycophron would return to Corinth and take up the tyranny. In order to avoid having Periander come to their city, says Herodotus, the Corcyreans murdered Lycophron, and earned the hatred of Periander (Hdt. 3.49–53). The presentation of this story conveys certain ideas about the tyranny. It emphasises the violent and destructive influence of tyranny on the family – Periander kills his wife and alienates his son, and the father-in-law causes the rift. It demonstrates Periander's fearsome reputation for cruelty, if the Corcyreans would resort to murder to keep him away, and in the terrible punishment which he inflicted on the city. Most of all, it implies that this was the end of the tyranny, which was not the case. Nicolaus fr. 60 tells us that in fact Periander had a large extended family, as had Cypselus: when Lycophron was killed the rule passed to his nephew Psammetichos, son of the tyrant of Ambracia, who returned to Corinth and governed under the name Cypselus II. Herodotus' story is clearly meant to make us think of tyranny as undesirable and self-defeating.

The role of Persia

Why did Herodotus shape his stories of tyranny to such negative effect? The main aim of his *Histories* was to record the war between the Greeks and the Persians, tracing the origins of their conflict from the earliest contacts; Herodotus is often called the first historian of the Western tradition, because as well as relating events he tried to explain the underlying patterns of cause and effect. The Persian Wars were indeed hard to understand: what motivated the Persians to attack Greece, when it offered so little potential reward, and what made the united Greek army able to defeat so vast an enemy? Herodotus tried to find answers to these questions, and therefore represented the opposition between Greece and Persia as fundamentally a clash of constitutions, between the monarchical

Persians and the self-governing Greeks. It is this which he offers as
an explanation for the extraordinary victory of the Greeks in the
face of overwhelming odds: they won because of their attachment to
freedom and law. His theory is made explicit in a scene between the
Persian King Xerxes and the Spartan Demaratus, who has defected
to the Persian side. Xerxes asks Demaratus whether the Greeks will
fight his army, or whether they will simply recognise their weakness
in the face of his invasion and surrender. Demaratus replies that the
Greeks, particularly the Spartans, will fight against any odds rather
than be enslaved, which Xerxes finds hard to believe: perhaps they
could be forced to fight by their commander, he says, or whipped
into battle, but a free man would not willingly face a thousand
opponents. Demaratus' statement of Spartan motivation makes the
difference between Greece and Persia plain:

> They are free, but not completely so, for they have a master
> whose name is Law, and they fear him even more than your
> subjects fear you. They do whatever he orders them, and the
> order is always the same: not to flee from battle, even in the
> face of vast numbers, but to stand firm in the battle line and
> win or die.

> (Hdt. 7.104.4–5)

For Herodotus the reason for Greek success was their attachment
to freedom and their willingness to fight for it, and his treatment
of tyranny is intended to tell the same story. That Greek states had
experienced tyranny was obvious, but he is keen to describe how
the Greeks had resisted the rule of tyrants and overthrown them;
he demonstrates in every case that tyranny is an evil both for the
state and for the individual concerned, and like Polycrates, fated to
fail. For the sake of his argument, no state can be seen to prosper
under a tyrant; he associates military and political success with the
abstract values of freedom and *isonomia* (equality before the law):

The Athenians now increased in strength, and showed that equality is an excellent thing, not in one way only, but in all ways, since while the Athenians were ruled by tyrants they were no more successful in war than any of their neighbours, but once the tyrants had been expelled they became by far the strongest.

(Hdt. 5.78)

This explains both why Herodotus is so keen to mention tyranny, and why he focuses on the overthrow of tyrants and the end of their rule.

Persia in this scheme of things is depicted as a tyranny under its King, with unwilling and servile subjects, and as a creator of tyrannies in the areas which it ruled. But the idea that Persia deliberately supported the ideology of tyranny is open to question, as can be seen from events in Ionia. The Greek states of the Ionian islands and Asia (modern Turkey) were considered by the mainland Greeks as both part and not part of Greece. Ionia had been settled in the great migrations of the tenth century, and the *poleis* here shared the same culture and gods as the mainland states, yet the Ionians were seen as different, more Eastern, luxury-loving and less hardy. This was partly because the cities had not retained their independence, having become subject to Croesus, the king of Lydia, in 560. In 546 the Lydian kingdom fell in turn to Persia under their empire-builder, Cyrus the Great, and the Greek states which had previously paid tribute to Croesus now became subjects of the Persian empire. At the end of the sixth century most Ionian states were ruled by tyrants. The *Histories* lists at least fifteen rulers, including Histiaeus of Miletus, Coes of Mytilene, Aeaces II of Samos, Aristagoras of Cyzicus and Ariston of Byzantium. Histiaeus, who led the Ionian cities in revolt from Persia in 499, claims that each of these nobles 'ruled their city through the power of Darius, and if

Darius were to be overthrown ... every city would prefer to be ruled as a democracy than as a tyranny' (Hdt. 4.137–8), which raises the question of how far these were naturally occurring tyrannies, and how far political appointments by the Persian administration. The Persian empire covered a huge area and had a complex bureaucracy; its territory was divided for administrative purposes into *satrapies*, each of which had a *satrap* (governor) responsible for collecting tribute, administering justice and military affairs. Given its extended lines of communication (it was three months' journey from the coast in Ionia to the capital at Susa) Persians favoured individual rulers in the states and cities which they controlled as easiest to deal with, and as a system where loyalty could easily be assured. They would deal with democracies or oligarchies when necessary, but preferred to encourage or impose sole rulers: an illustration of their techniques is given by the experience of Themistocles, the Greek general who defected to Persia in 469. He found favour with King Artaxerxes who gave him the revenues of three cities, Magnesia for his bread, Lampsacus for his wine and Myus for his meat, as it was said. Coins recently found in the area with a portrait seem to show Themistocles installed as ruler, and the suggestion of Histiaeus is that states in Ionia had been 'given' to their tyrants in the same way.[31]

As with the mainland tyrannies, however, Herodotus' account is ideologically motivated. Ionia was important to his project because of the events of the 490s, when the Ionian states made an ill-fated attempt to break free from Persia. They received only half-hearted support from Athens – Sparta refused to aid them at all – and were rapidly subjected again, but the rebellion's ideological implications were more significant to Herodotus than its practical results. As an initial declaration of independence from Persia, the ringleader Aristagoras abdicated his rule at Miletus in favour of a democracy, and encouraged all the other cities to remove their tyrants at the

same time. Democracies were set up across Ionia and the tyrants
overthrown. This makes for a neat equation – tyrants under Persia,
democracies when free – but to say this is an oversimplification.
Not every tyranny had been established by Persia, as the example
of Polycrates demonstrates – he and his brothers took power from
within. Several rulers, too, were of long standing: Lygdamis of
Naxos, for instance, had assisted Pisistratus into power in 560, long
before the Persians came. Nor were all the Ionian rulers clear-cut
tyrants; some had characteristics more like hereditary kings. An
intriguing example of this is the tyrant of Herodotus' own home
town, Halicarnassus, whom he described in some detail. Artemisia
I had become ruler of Halicarnassus on her husband's death, and it
was obviously a source of consternation to the Greeks that a woman
should rule, and that she should take part in Xerxes' invasion of
Greece as she did, acting as advisor to the King and leading a
contingent of warships (Hdt. 7.99). But the striking feature about
Artemisia, apart from her courage and military prowess, is that she
had inherited power as sole ruler even though she had an adult son.
Evidently power in this family passed down the female line: the son
could not inherit until his mother abdicated or died. This practice
is known in other Eastern dynasties, and suggests that the Ionians
had combined native traditions with *polis* habits. Ionian and Persian
attitudes towards tyranny were also more complex than Herodotus
implies: although the tyrants were expelled as a preliminary to the
revolt, the process seems to have been largely bloodless – only Coes
at Mytilene was killed by an angry populace, and the other tyrants
departed peacefully (Hdt. 5.38). The Persian response reveals them
to lack any ideological commitment to particular constitutions: when
the revolt failed, tyrants were restored in most Ionian cities, including
Aeaces at Samos, but a few years later, when the Persian general
Mardonius came through Ionia on his way to Marathon, he deposed
the tyrants once more and replaced them with democratic regimes

(Hdt. 6.43). The Persians, unsurprisingly, made their interventions on pragmatic grounds, and would encompass any regime within their empire if it offered them an advantage to do so.

The 'end of tyranny'

By the end of the fifth century there came to be a conviction that tyranny had ended by 480 BC with both mainland and Ionian rulers overthrown. The idea of an organised 'end of tyranny' is expressed in Thucydides' formulation of early Greek history which, as we have seen, was very influential. He says that the Spartans put down tyranny in the rest of Greece shortly before the battle of Marathon in 490, and this idea of a deliberate campaign by the Spartans to depose tyrants in the *poleis* of the Peloponnese and southern Greece is followed up in later writers, notably Plutarch, who gave a full list of the tyrannies which the Spartans ended:

> Was it merely for the sake of a breastplate or a mixing-bowl that the Spartans expelled the Cypselids from Corinth and Ambracia, Lygdamis from Naxos, the sons of Pisistratus from Athens, Aeschines from Sicyon, Symmachus from Thasos, Aulis from Phocis and Aristogenes from Miletus, and besides put an end to the *dynasteia* in Thessaly, when King Leotychidas ousted Aristomedes and Agelaus?
>
> (Plut. *On the Malice of Herodotus* 859)

This shows every sign of a story which has been built up over time: the Spartans did indeed get rid of the Pisistratids under their king Cleomenes, but the other interventions are harder to validate. Aristotle, for instance, says that the tyranny at Ambracia was overthrown in a democratic uprising, and there is no indication either in Herodotus or Nicolaus of Spartan involvement in the ending of the Cypselid dynasty at Corinth. Sparta is credited with bringing about the fall of Aeschines at Sicyon in a fragment of papyrus which says that the overthrow took place at the same time as the exiling of Hippias from Athens, but it is difficult to reconcile this with previous Spartan policy towards Sicyon, which had always been favourable to the tyrants. The other rulers are known only from this passage of Plutarch, and a conclusion is therefore impossible. Andrewes speaks of a 'crusade against tyranny in favour of constitutional government', but this builds too much on limited evidence. Even the intervention in Athens was hardly motivated by political idealism, since Herodotus says that as soon as the Spartans realised that they had been tricked into opposing the Pisistratids, they reversed their decision and tried to recall Hippias into power, as their relationship with the Athenian tyrants had always been friendly.[32] But once the idea of Sparta as an opponent of tyranny had been established, one can see how other episodes could easily be attributed to them.

Did tyranny really come to an end after 500, Spartans or not? The tyrants of the Peloponnese and the islands had followed one another into power, and indeed helped each other to gain and keep it, so it may be that the fall of one had an effect on the others. It is true that we see fewer mainland tyrannies in the fifth century, but this is partly an effect of our sources: Herodotus (and Plutarch) give the impression that all tyrannies came to an end at the same time, which was certainly not the case with some of the most powerful dynasties of the period, those of Sicily and Italy.

The Western Mediterranean may seem marginal to the history of Greece and Ionia, but Sicily and Italy were neither separate from Greece nor insignificant. The cities of Magna Graecia – Naxos, Syracuse, Gela, Leontini and Rhegium, among others – were founded in the wave of Greek migration from 700, and the settlements proved so successful that the new foundations in many cases produced further colonies of their own, Acragas from Gela, for instance, and Camarina from Syracuse (Thuc. 6.3–5). The Sicilian and Italian states were very wealthy, commanding both resources and trade routes, and retained strong ties with the mainland. Links between colony and mother-state were always strong: citizens of the new *polis* turned to their metropolis for help in political or military crises, received new settlers from there, and participated in both local and panhellenic festivals. These settlements, like those of the mainland, developed tyrannies from the very beginning of their history. Rulers such as Pantaleon of Leontini are little more than names to us, but Phalaris of Acragas (570–554) stands out more clearly in the pages of history, even though the only act for which he was really remembered by the Greeks was one of extreme cruelty and extravagance, the creation of the bronze bull in which he used to roast his enemies alive. This entered the public consciousness in an indelible way; Pindar's *First Pythian Ode* uses him as the archetype of the bad ruler:

> The kindly generosity of Croesus does not fade; but a hateful story is forever told of Phalaris, pitiless in mind, who burned his victims in the brazen bull. He is no theme for lyres beneath the roof and gentle choirs of boys in their songs.
>
> (ll.93–8)

Polybius (12.25) says that the bull was taken from Acragas to Carthage in 406 BC, and Diodorus (13.90.4) that many years later when the Romans destroyed Carthage in 146, a bronze bull was found and restored to Acragas. The tyrants who followed, though nowhere near as inventively cruel, proved to be some of the most notable of all time; even Thucydides, who tried to minimise the achievements of tyranny, gives them grudging notice:

> Because the tyrants in Greece looked solely to their own interests, both of personal comfort and the increase of their family's reputation, they made safety the greatest goal of their

rule, and consequently nothing of any note was achieved by them, unless it was to do with their local interests. Only the tyrants in Sicily came to be particularly powerful.

(Thuc. 1.17)

The first rulers of real note were Cleander and his brother Hippocrates who ruled in succession at Gela, and succeeded in bringing many towns in eastern Sicily under Gelan rule. After Hippocrates' death one of his cavalry commanders, Gelon son of Deinomenes, usurped power from Hippocrates' sons and took over Gela; he then went on to capture Syracuse, the most important Sicilian *polis*, and made it his centre of operations. Herodotus relates that a revolution had taken place in which the Syracusan *demos* had enlisted the help of their slaves and thrown out the landowners; Gelon intervened on the side of the aristocrats and used the opportunity to take control of the city (an episode which sits badly with the image of the tyrant as a champion of the people, and illustrates the varying circumstances which could give rise to tyrants). Gelon then put his brother Hieron in charge of Gela and moved his centre of rule to Syracuse, which he increased in size by adding population from Camarina, Megara Hyblaea and Sicilian Euboea, all of which he had captured, making Syracuse into the largest *polis* of his time (Hdt. 7.153–6). He shared his rule with his three brothers Hieron, Polyzalus and Thrasyboulus, placing all three in positions of authority and setting up an intricate system of intermarriages with other Italian dynasties. Gelon married Damareta, daughter of the powerful Theron of Acragas, while Hieron married his niece; Theron himself married Polyzalos' daughter. Hieron was also married to the daughter of Anaxilas of Rhegium in Italy, creating a web of obligations between these powerful families.

Gelon's finest hour was his successful defence of Greek Sicily against an invading Carthaginian army of 300,000 under Hamilcar

in 478. Although the invasion was really about local politics –
Terillus, tyrant of Himera, had been deposed by Theron of Acragas
and requested aid from his connections in Carthage to restore
himself; Gelon was drawn into the conflict as the ally of Theron
– Gelon seized the opportunity to equate his struggle with the
Greek defence against the Persian invasion which took place at
the same time. He encouraged the idea that his victory over the
Carthaginian forces at the river Himera had taken place on the
same day as the Greeks' victory at Salamis (Hdt. 7.165–6). Gelon
was clearly concerned to foster his reputation at home and abroad:
Diodorus knows a story of his childhood, which was presumably
told to emphasise that he was destined for greatness:

> As a boy he was sitting in school when a wolf appeared and
> snatched his writing-tablet from him. While he was chasing
> after the wolf and his tablet, the school was shaken by an
> earthquake and collapsed, killing all the other boys and their
> teacher.
>
> (Diod. 10.29)

and he set up lavish dedications in the religious centres of Greece
to draw attention to his achievements, a monument at Delphi
commemorating the victory at Himera, and a treasury at Olympia
housing dedications from the battle.[33]

This campaign came towards the end of his life, but his reign
had been a long and successful one. As well as making Syracuse
strong and prosperous, he had retained the support of his subjects:
Diodorus (11. 26.4–7) tells us that after Himera he presented
himself unarmed before the Syracusan assembly and submitted
himself to their judgement of his actions; far from trying to deprive
him of power, the assembly hailed him as 'Saviour and Benefactor
and King'. The language is anachronistic – Diodorus is clearly
interpreting Gelon's action through the prism of Hellenistic kingship

and its titles – but Sicilian tyranny did have a distinctly different flavour from that on the mainland. It has been suggested that Gelon and his family did in fact call themselves kings in Sicily, and their actions, transplanting populations and founding or moving cities, were on a grand scale.[34]

After Gelon's death in 478 Hieron duly succeeded to the tyranny, marrying his brother's wife Damareta in a symbolic continuation of the reign. Hieron is noted for two things in particular: his role as patron of the arts, and his alleged institution of a spy service. He is the dedicatee of several victory odes by Pindar and Bacchylides, composed to celebrate his victories in the horse- and chariot-races at Olympia and Delphi, including the *First Pythian Ode*, quoted above, on the occasion of his victory in the chariot-race at Delphi in 470; he also commissioned a play from Aeschylus, the *Women of Aetna*, for the celebrations marking his foundation of a new city at Aetna, near Catana. The only story which Aristotle preserves about him is more sinister – that he employed a corps of spies, called Listeners, whom he would send to meetings or gatherings of the people, to make sure that he knew of any plots or subversion. But spies or no, Hieron enjoyed as favourable a reputation as his brother, ruled until 467, and was succeeded by the third Deinomenid brother, Thrasyboulus.[35]

The Deinomenids are tyrants of a familiar type, conquering territory and building monuments, but were also consciously archaic in some ways, with their multiple marriages, grandiose foundation of cities and movements of populations. They were not an isolated phenomenon in Magna Graecia but existed in a wider context of Western tyranny. As we have seen there were other powerful ruling families at Acragas in Sicily and in the cities on the toe of Italy, such as Rhegium. At Cumae in Italy the tyrant Aristodemus 'the Effeminate' ruled between 504 and 490, nor were tyrant-like rulers confined to Greek states at this period: we can see strong similarities with figures in Etruria, such as Thefarie Velinas, 'king' of Caere, who is referred to as some kind of chief magistrate, yet held sole power for life, and perhaps also Lars Porsenna, king of Clusium. The last two kings of Rome, Servius Tullius and Tarquinius Superbus, are depicted in Greek and Roman sources as tyrants, usurping power rather than gaining it legitimately, and modern scholarship has recently moved towards seeing their tyranny as genuine, influenced by contemporary contacts with Greece, and not just a later historians' invention.[36]

Many of these tyrannical families fell from power in the 470s and 460s: Theron's son Thrasydaeus had been expelled from Acragas by Hieron in 477, Thrasyboulus was ousted from Syracuse in 466 after a reign of less than a year, and the sons of Anaxilas were expelled from Rhegium in 461. This has been interpreted as the last gasp of tyranny as it disappeared from Sicily, rather later than from mainland Greece but in the same way. But Sicilian tyranny did not die – it was to be surprisingly durable. A limited democracy (described by Aristotle as a *politeia*, a mixed constitution between oligarchy and democracy) was established at Syracuse, but proved to be very vulnerable to internal factionism.[37] The struggle between rich and poor was difficult to resolve, each side fearing the consequences of the political supremacy of the other, and under the pressure of warfare and invasion in the 410s the Syracusan democracy was found to be seriously wanting. Tyranny answered the needs of the *poleis* in Sicily since it tended to originate in military command, allowed the creation of unity across a diverse population, and could offer the security and continuity which was felt to be lacking from more popular governments. Syracuse, and Sicily, were to be ruled by remarkable tyrants for most of the rest of their history.

Tyranny in the fifth century

If there was no 'end of tyranny' in the West and East, was there really an end to it in the mainland *poleis*? Many modern writers have painted tyranny as an 'immature' phase of political development which was naturally superseded by more inclusive forms of rule, and believe that with the advent of democracy in Athens tyranny ceased to be a realistic prospect here or elsewhere in Greece. This belief is again, however, a consequence of our sources. For events after 479 we depend on Thucydides, who narrowed the focus of his work to concentrate on events involving just Athens and Sparta for the next seventy years. Hence we know little of the internal politics of any *polis* outside Athens. Once the reforms of Cleisthenes had been passed in 508, Athens itself was resolutely democratic, yet even here we can detect a continuing anxiety about tyrants and tyranny. We have seen how the Athenians developed a myth of resistance to tyranny in the course of the fifth century, suggesting that the citizens had deposed the tyrants themselves, and it became normal to assert that the tyrants had been alone in grasping at power, while all other families of note had opposed them. These were, after all, the ancestors of the men who later became important under the democracy, and their political credentials had to be sound. The Alcmaeonids, the most prominent Athenian family in the fifth century, had, it was said, been in exile during the Pisistratid tyranny, and had returned only to effect their overthrow. This seemed to establish them firmly as opponents of tyranny, but the discovery in the 1930s of a fragment of the list of Athenian *archons* threw this claim into confusion. Cleisthenes the Alcmaeonid was revealed to have held the *archonship* in 525/4, something which could only have happened with the favour of Hippias, and the story of the exile was revealed to be a later fabrication, designed to distance members of the family from a connection with an embarrassing past. In fact it is plain that the Alcmaeonids had a long history of involvement with tyranny: the founder of the family, Alcmaeon, originally gained his fortune from Croesus the king of Lydia; his son Megacles was the Athenian who married Cleisthenes of Sicyon's daughter, and who later helped Pisistratus into power (with a bargain about power-sharing); his descendant held the *archonship* under Pisistratid rule. After the fall of the tyrants, however, this same Cleisthenes went on to challenge for primacy as a democratic reformer, and his descendant Pericles became the leader of the democracy after 460. We can detect a competition of histories here: members of the family seem to have been consistently open to accusations of desiring tyranny, and to have created a myth of opposition to it in their defence.[38]

Despite these efforts to consign the Pisistratids to history, tyranny remained a preoccupation at Athens. Early on there was a real prospect of the restoration of Hippias or his sons – the Spartans proposed returning him to power around 500 when they discovered how they had been tricked into overthrowing him, and when they were vetoed by their Peloponnesian allies, Hippias forged links with Persia, and accompanied the Persian army when they invaded at Marathon in 490, hoping to be restored under Persian rule (Hdt. 6.106–7). And although the democracy established in 508 proved very stable, precautions about tyranny remained. Condemnation had been passed on the family of Pisistratus, but suspicion lingered about other Athenians: the general Miltiades was prosecuted in 493 for having held a tyranny in the Chersonnese, and a group identified as 'friends of the tyrants' were active into the 480s. The Athenians were similarly wary of letting in tyrants in the states of their empire: when they drew up regulations for Erythrae after its conquest in the 450s directing how the state should be run, they included a regulation sentencing to death anyone who should 'betray the city to the tyrants'.[39] Suggestions that an individual

might wish to establish a tyranny were never far from the surface
in Athenian politics: they were levelled at Pericles, pre-eminent in
politics in the 440s and 430s, whose complete control of affairs
through his personal authority made many uncomfortable, and at
Alcibiades, another of the Alcmaeonid line, who was exiled from
Athens in 415 because, says Thucydides, he was thought to be
aiming at a tyranny.

> He had a great reputation among the citizens, and his enthusiasm
> for horse-breeding and other extravagances went beyond what
> his property could supply ... most people were frightened by the
> scale of his lawlessness in his private life, and the spirit in which
> he carried out whatever he did, and so they turned against him,
> believing that he wished to become tyrant.
>
> (Thuc. 6.15)

How realistic were these fears? A debate centres on a famous passage
in Aristophanes' comedy *Wasps*. *Wasps* was first performed in 426, a
few years after the beginning of Athens' war against Sparta, a time
of great fear and anxiety as the Spartans invaded Attica and laid
waste to the farms. In the play the main character, Bdelycleon, talks
about the atmosphere of suspicion within the city:

> Everything with you people is 'tyranny' and conspirators',
> If anyone criticises anything, large or small.
> I haven't even heard the word 'tyranny' for fifty years,
> But now it's as common as salted fish,
> And you hear it everywhere in the Agora.
> If someone buys perch and doesn't want sprats
> Straight away the sprat-seller nearby says
> 'This man seems to buy his fish like a tyrant!'
> Or if you ask for an onion as relish for your sardines,
> The vegetable-woman gives you a nasty look and says,

'You're asking for an onion: do you want to be a tyrant –
Do you think that Athens should pay you tribute in
seasonings?'

(ll. 488–99)

Obviously this is a comedy, but it seems to indicate that fears of
tyranny had returned in the 420s. Was it no more than political
rhetoric? Many scholars believe so, though mainly because they
know that tyranny was not to return to Athens until much later: the
threat which faced the democracy was of a different nature, a coup
by an oligarchic junta, the Four Hundred. But this does not mean
that Athenians in the 420s and 410s did not fear the emergence
of a tyrant, and although we know only the political events that
Thucydides chose to tell, there is the occasional indication that
tyranny had not vanished. In 431, for instance, a tyrant called
Euarchus was ruling in the Acarnanian *polis* of Astacus; he was
removed from power by the Athenians, but reinstated shortly
afterwards by the Corinthians (Thuc. 2.30, 33). This is our only
mention of Euarchus, so we cannot tell how long he had held
power or how long his rule lasted, but the episode indicates that
tyrants were still present, and close to home. Although Thucydides
presents the Peloponnesian War as an ideological contest between
democracy and oligarchy, the citizens of Athens in 415 still saw
tyranny as an equally likely prospect (Thuc. 6.60). The Athenians
gave their own answer to the question when they redrafted their
law against the subversion of the constitution in 410: after the Four
Hundred gave up power and the democracy was restored, a decree
was passed which required all Athenians to take an oath: 'I will kill
... anyone who overthrows the democracy at Athens, anyone who
holds public office after the constitution has been overthrown, and
anyone who establishes himself as a tyrant or joins in setting up a
tyrant.' (Andoc. 2.97). Evidently Athenians at the end of the fifth

century did not consider tyranny an archaic form of rule which had died out: they sought to protect themselves from it as a serious proposition.[40]

This chapter has shown how the myth of the 'end of tyranny' was formed, and the elements which supported it – Spartan claims to be the enemies of tyrants, the identification of tyranny with Persia, and the importance of anti-tyrannical rhetoric in Athenian politics. All of these factors influenced historians writing in the period, who tended to direct their gaze away from the successful tyrants of their time. But although the fifth-century Greeks liked to present tyranny as something foreign or archaic to which they were thoroughly opposed, tyrants continued to rule and flourish across the Greek world. And instead of bringing an end to tyranny, the years after 410 were to usher in a new era of famous and powerful rulers.

CHAPTER 3

TYRANNY REMADE?

Dionysius I, tyrant of Syracuse, *archon* of Sicily, is the tyrant's tyrant. Many of the truly great tyrant stories – the Sword of Damocles, Damon and Pythias – are his, as are outrageous tales of paranoia: for example, too fearful to allow a barber to shave him with a razor, he is said to have trained his daughters to singe off his beard with red-hot walnut shells. One of the most telling stories in his tradition concerns his poetic activities: Dionysius wrote verse, and those who gathered at his court were expected to admire it. One of his guests, the poet Philoxenus of Cythera, criticised some particularly bad drama, and as punishment was sent to labour in the stone quarries in Syracuse. The next day Dionysius relented, and invited Philoxenus to dinner again; he read more of his poetry, and asked Philoxenus what he thought of it this time. Philoxenus immediately turned to the slaves and said, 'Back to the quarry, then!' Dionysius, we are told, forgave him because of the joke, but Philoxenus eventually found a successful strategy to cope with the difficult situation: whenever asked for his opinion of one of Dionysius' verses, he would say simply, 'Pitiful! Pitiful!' Dionysius, interpreting this as a comment on the emotional effect of his work, was satisfied, while Philoxenus was saved from having to lie about his opinion.[41]

The story has several layers of meaning. It shows the combination of power and insecurity with which Dionysius is credited by many ancient writers; it reveals his aspirations to excel in areas other than the military; it demonstrates the attempts by the mainland Greek states to belittle Dionysius in the areas that they could; and the moral is of course that power cannot buy either talent or the respect of your peers. One can draw modern parallels with the tales told in the West of Saddam Hussein's novels, or Kim Il Jong's golfing exploits. The story makes Dionysius seem unimpressive, even ridiculous, and this too is purposeful, distracting the fourth-century Greeks from the uncomfortable reality of his wealth and influence.

The years between 410 and 320 are dominated by some of the greatest of all tyrants – the Dionysii at Syracuse, the Hecatomnids in Caria, and Jason and his descendants in Thessaly – as well as a large number of more minor figures. These fourth-century tyrants are usually represented as significantly different in nature from the rulers of the archaic period. They were not, it is suggested, the grand and wealthy figures that Cleisthenes and Polycrates had been, but adventurers and opportunists, given a route to power by the social changes which followed the Peloponnesian War. Scholars point to the ready availability of mercenary troops, the numbers of which had expanded as a consequence of the war, and to the growing importance of money in political life. A man who controlled a source of wealth could easily buy himself an army with which to take power. Consequently it is also suggested that tyrants in the fourth century were less closely linked to political unrest than their predecessors: an aspiring tyrant no longer needed the support of the *demos*, since he could manufacture his own support. Hence they were not populist leaders but self-serving oppressors, resented by the citizens over whom they ruled and rightly fearful of rebellion or assassination. And finally the claim is frequently made that tyrannies appeared at this time on the fringes of the Greek world, in areas which were less 'advanced' than the mainland states. This chapter will examine some of the most famous tyrannies to see whether these claims are valid. A significant difference to note at the

outset is that the evidence on which we can draw for the rulers of
this period is often contemporary, and therefore much more direct
and detailed: in contrast to Herodotus, who was writing about rulers
hundreds of years before his time, historians like Xenophon wrote
about events at which they had been present, and people whom they
knew. This can make their histories one-sided, but it gives us a much
better insight into what contemporaries thought and said about the
rulers of their age. So what makes a tyrant in this period, and how
did the concept relate to what had gone before?

Dionysius of Syracuse

Dionysius' rise to power was as a textbook usurper tyrant; his rule
had its origin, as had that of the Deinomenids, in a Carthaginian
attack on Sicily, and although Diodorus suggests that Dionysius
had plotted to take power by undermining the generals in charge of
the defence of Syracuse, his original appointment was a legitimate
one: the assembly appointed him *strategos autocrator* (general with
supreme authority) to take charge of the war on the strength of his
military expertise. Dionysius then, we are told, surrounded himself
with armed supporters and mercenaries, set up his headquarters
in the harbour and proclaimed himself tyrant (Diod. 13.92-6).
Diodorus' account, hostile though it is in tone, nevertheless makes
clear that Dionysius did not lack support among the citizens. An
abortive uprising in 405 was led by the cavalry (comprising the
aristocratic class), but collapsed when the mass of citizens refused
to lend their aid (Diod. 13.112). Early on in his reign Dionysius gave
grants of land and houses to the *demos* and to slaves whom he had
enfranchised as 'New Citizens', and he is said to have won over the
people after further unrest in 396 by 'kind words, gifts, and inviting
them to public banquets' (Diod. 14.7.4-5, 14.70.3). Throughout
his career various episodes of unrest are recorded, but Dionysius'

reorganisation of the city, including the creation of a fortified palace complex on the island of Ortygia, and his expansionist policies meant benefits for the ordinary Syracusans, if not for the aristocracy. His initial power came from the assembly, and the assembly continued to play a role throughout his reign – we see him putting decisions on war or peace to the vote – but Dionysius also surrounded himself with his family, appointing his brothers Thearidas and Leptines and his brothers-in-law Dion and Polyxenos to key positions as admirals, ambassadors and generals. He associated his sons with himself as rulers and clearly aimed to establish a lasting dynasty.[42]

Once in control Dionysius built a huge fortress on the island of Ortygia off the city itself, a veritable town-within-a-town, including houses for all his intimate friends and barracks for his soldiers. He retained his mercenaries to enforce his power, according to his detractors, but also because he had very large territorial ambitions. From Syracuse he gradually extended his control of the Greek cities until he controlled the whole of eastern Sicily and then made preparations for a war against Carthage. He invited craftsmen from Italy, Greece and Africa to Syracuse and created a 'workshop of war', encouraging rivalry and invention and producing all kinds of arms and armour, new and bigger ships and the first torsion catapult (Diod. 14.41–3). With the help of the latter he captured the key Carthaginian fort of Motya in 397 and by 396 had driven the Carthaginians to the very margins of the island, leaving him in effective control of Sicily. After 392 there was peace in Sicily for a decade, and Dionysius turned his gaze outward to Italy, taking Rhegium and Caulonia and even launching a campaign in Tyrrhenia. The Carthaginian threat never entirely went away, however, and for the rest of his reign Dionysius tried to oust the Carthaginians from Sicily, never with complete success – supposedly because he had been warned by an oracle that he would die when he had conquered 'his betters' (Diod. 15.74). Believing this to refer to

Carthage, Dionysius never pursued a campaign to ultimate victory, and was always willing to make peace and maintain the division of territory within Sicily. A story like this was obviously circulated to account for Dionysius' behaviour in the face of complaints that he never managed to vanquish Carthage decisively, and may have been intended to counteract suggestions about the cynical use of war to keep the citizens in subjection, though in fact Carthage was simply too strong. Further afield Dionysius founded colonies at Lissus and Pharos on the Illyrian coast with the intention of controlling the Ionian Sea, creating concern in Greece at the potential scale of his ambition: Diodorus (15.13) says that his ultimate aim was to attack Epirus, which may have been true, and to sack the temple at Delphi and seize the treasures, which is extremely unlikely – such an act would have horrified the Greek world, although it is a motivation often attributed to the tyrants of the age.

The Greek attitude towards Dionysius was contradictory: despite engaging in anti-tyrannical rhetoric both Athens and Sparta courted Dionysius as an ally. Sparta actually intervened twice in the early years of his rule to help him maintain power, in one case refusing to help an attempted uprising by the Syracusan *demos*. In return, once his power was firmly established, Dionysius sent ships and troops to aid the Spartans in their wars in 373 and again in 369/8. The Athenians were equally interested in gaining Dionysius as an ally: inscriptions survive indicating that they pursued his favour for some time, granting honours to him and his brothers in 393, bestowing citizenship on him and his sons in 369 and ultimately achieving an alliance in 368.[43] Obviously the Greek states wanted to exploit Dionysius' military resources, both ships and soldiers, for use in the constant warfare which obtained at this time, and in exchange for his contributions Dionysius gained reputation and standing in the mainland, a matter about which he cared a great deal. He had striven from the beginning for recognition and acceptance in the wider

Greek world: following the practice of his Deinomenid predecessors he sent magnificent offerings to be presented at the Olympic Games in 388 under the care of his brother Thearidas. Greek ambivalence towards Dionysius is shown by their reaction to this display: the orator Lysias made an inflammatory speech (the *Olympic Oration*) depicting him as a tyrant and an enemy of Greek freedom, as a result of which the audience turned on Dionysius' envoys and tore down their magnificent pavilion. Dionysius also made dedications at Delphi and Olympia and did his best to attract major Greek writers and philosophers to his court, among whom of course was Plato (discussed further in the next chapter). The description of his court which appears in Plato's *Letters* shows us a huge array of intellectual guests, with Dionysius keen to make Syracuse the cultural centre of the Mediterranean. He also entered dramatic and poetic festivals at Athens, winning a prize in the dramatic festival of the Lenaia in 367 with his play *The Ransom of Hector*.

The orchestration of public opinion was something to which Dionysius paid as much attention as to his military preparations and campaigns. An Athenian source, for instance, reports the story that:

> a woman from Himera dreamed that she was taken up to the heavens and shown the dwellings of the gods. There she saw Zeus sitting on his throne, at the foot of which was a huge red man bound in chains. She asked her guide who he was, and he said, 'This is the bane of Sicily and Italy, and if he is ever released, he will destroy these places.' Some time later she chanced to meet Dionysius with his bodyguards, and when she saw him she shouted out that he was the bane she had been shown, and fainted dead away. Three months later she disappeared, having been secretly murdered by Dionysius.
>
> (Schol. Aesch. 2.10)

Dionysius employed a court historian and launched his own stories to counter the doom-laden tales: it was said, for instance, that just before becoming tyrant Dionysius was out hunting one day and lost his horse while crossing a river. He had given up any hope of finding it when it re-emerged from the wood with a swarm of bees nesting in its mane, indicating the future success of his plans. There are suggestions that even the 'red man' story may have existed in a parallel positive version, with Dionysius identified as the bane of Carthage, not of his own country. He also made capital from his wives and children, celebrating not one but two marriages in 398, one to the Syracusan Aristomache and one to the foreigner Doris, from Locri in Italy. The marriages were celebrated with ostentation – one bride arrived in a quinquireme with gold and silver fittings, the other in a chariot drawn by four white horses – and were consummated on the same night, with Dionysius keeping secret which of the women he slept with first, to ensure that his wives were equal in status. He proceeded to establish two parallel families, and in the next generation married his daughters (provocatively named Dikaiosyne (Justice), Sophrosyne (Prudence) and Arete (Virtue)) within the extended family. Sophrosyne, who was the daughter of Aristomache, became the wife of the heir Dionysius the Younger (son of Doris), while Dikaiosyne married her uncle Leptines and Arete her uncle Dion. The point of such an unusual family structure was first to emphasise the uniqueness of the tyrant – to have two wives and a family which married only within itself marked him out as beyond normal expectations and behaviour – and perhaps also to align himself with figures of myth, who were also beyond normal social structures (Zeus and Hera, for example, were brother and sister as well as husband and wife). Like the earlier tyrants, Dionysius wanted to show that he was fated to rule.[44]

Dionysius met his end in a suitably colourful way: when his play won first prize in the dramatic contest at Athens he drank himself to death during the lavish celebrations (Diod. 15.74). Historians disapproved, seeing it as one more indictment of his luxurious and uncontrolled lifestyle, but it was in fact a very positive end, the warlike tyrant dying at home after forty years of rule and handing on power to his son. More than any other tyrant Dionysius' reputation suffered in subsequent ages (for reasons we shall see), but the colourful stories and 'black legend' should not be allowed to eclipse his long and successful reign.

Thessalian tyranny

Dionysius, easily understood as a classic tyrant in the archaic mould, contrasts with his mainland contemporary Jason of Pherae, who came to dominate the affairs of Greece in the 370s. Jason was from Thessaly in the north of Greece, a region which had hitherto been something of a backwater. Although rich in agricultural land – Thessaly was the historic home of Greece's best horses – it was less urbanised than the southern states. It was traditionally divided into four regions, called tetrads, linked in a federation of sorts, together with several independent *poleis*, of which Pherae, home of Jason, was one. Usually the tetrads and *poleis* acted independently, but in wartime they could unite themselves under one ruler, called the *tagos* or warlord. Notable *tagoi* of the past had tended to be drawn from a small number of aristocratic families, suggesting a rather Homeric approach to political power.[45]

When Jason first appears in our histories in 375 he is already in the process of uniting the four tetrads under his rule, intimidating the *polis* of Pharsalus into submission, and about to claim control of all of Thessaly (Xen. *Hell.* 6.1). The key to his success was his large and well-organised mercenary army, and Xenophon writes extensively about his sound leadership and military innovation. Not only was a force of mercenaries tougher and better trained than a citizen army, Jason used novel techniques such as night manoeuvres and sudden advances. He rewarded his men with extra pay, medical attention and honours, and led by example, suffering hardship alongside them (Xen. *Hell.* 6.1.6, 15). With the loyalty of such a force, Jason effectively had a private army, although stories suggest that in the early days his ambition was not always matched by the necessary wealth: he is supposed to have resorted to a series of ruses for raising cash from his family, including trapping his brother in the bathhouse so he could use his signet ring to borrow money, and rushing into his mother's house pretending that his mercenary troops were threatening to kill him because their wages were unpaid, so that his mother would give him the money to save himself (Polyain. *Strat.* 6.2, 5).

Once he was recognised as *tagos* he controlled the resources of the whole country, giving him even greater manpower as well as tribute and taxation. After bringing all the cities of Thessaly under his control he expanded his reach into central Greece and the north by 371, making alliances with Thebes and Athens. 'No power on earth could afford to disregard him,' according to Xenophon, and there was a serious expectation that he would try to become 'tyrant of Greece' (Xen. *Hell.* 6.4.28, 32). In his ambition and campaigning success he has been compared to Alexander the Great, and there are some similarities: Jason was not a typical self-indulgent tyrant, aiming to enjoy luxury, feasting and sexual pleasure, but a man who valued military conquest above all else, and who was happy to share hardships with his soldiers. He is credited with ambitions to rival Alexander's: to take over the whole of Greece, and then perhaps to launch an attack on Persia. The orator Isocrates saw him as a potential leader for a panhellenic expedition against Persia, which suggests that talk of Jason's plans had spread far and wide. In 370 he prepared huge sacrifices for the Pythian Games at Delphi, and was suspected of aiming to take over the administration of the games – the Panhellenic games remained an ideal stage for the grand gesture – and of planning to steal the sacred treasures. It all came to nothing, however, because he was assassinated by a group of young men while holding a cavalry review (Xen. *Hell.* 6.4.31–2). Xenophon presents the motives of the assassins as straightforward liberation from tyranny, but it may have had more to do with internal Thessalian politics.

Jason can be (and is) categorised as a new type of tyrant, a freebooter lord, but the events following his death indicate that there is more to him than this. The question of his constitutional role is a difficult one. As *tagos* he was not technically a tyrant – it was an elected position. But the fact that he was succeeded by his brothers Polyphron and Polydorus as joint rulers (Xen. *Hell.* 6.4.33) suggests that he did not hold the *tageia* as a simple magistracy either; indeed it may be that Jason was himself related to a previous tyrant of Pherae, Lycophron, and thus making some claim to a hereditary power. The *tageia* by this stage was being held as more than a temporary command: it has been suggested that it was in fact an obsolete role which Jason had reinvented to describe his power. The uncertainty is shown by Xenophon's description of Jason's successors: Polydorus was soon killed and Polyphron ruled alone for a year, 'turning his *tageia* into a tyranny' by his violent and oppressive treatment of the Thessalians (6.4.34). He too was then murdered by Polydorus' son Alexander, who assumed the position of *tagos* while claiming to be 'putting an end to the tyranny' with the murder (6.4.35).[46]

Yet Alexander of Pherae is the member of the dynasty about whom our sources have the least doubt: he is consistently described as a tyrant, and gained a reputation as a monster, even figuring in Dante's *Inferno* (12.107) as an exemplar of extreme violence and cruelty. He appears in most Greek sources as a tyrannical cautionary tale, since he ended by being murdered by his own wife,

but the vision of a universally bad ruler, constantly struggling to
retain power and impose himself as tyrant on a reluctant populace
is not very convincing historically.[47] The political circumstances in
which he ruled were different from Jason's time – the Thessalians
now had powerful and interventionist neighbours in Thebes and
Macedonia. Alexander ruled for five years between 369 and 364, but
faced difficulty in maintaining his position because the other noble
families were less willing to accept him than they had been Jason,
and invited the Thebans to intervene and overthrow him. In the face
of such a threat, Thebes being the premier military power of the
day, Alexander did remarkably well, retaining his position as *tagos*
and at one stage capturing and imprisoning the Theban commander
Pelopidas, something which contributed to the historians' hostility
towards him (Plut. *Pel.* 27–8). There is no real sign, apart from
the lurid stories of Plutarch and Cicero, that Alexander was a
harsh or unpopular ruler – he presided over the fortification of
the country, exploited the harbour and trade to generate wealth,
and coined money. Even when the Thebans did oust him as *tagos*
in 364 he retained the rulership of Pherae and continued to seek
foreign alliances. Alexander could not create the consent to his
rule that Jason had done, but he was approved by Isocrates as a
potential panhellenic leader, suggesting that his qualities have been
overshadowed in our sources. Xenophon in fact discusses nothing
of his reign except on the murder story, complete with cinematic
touches (such as Thebe holding onto the doorknocker of the room to
prevent her husband escaping), but even this was not the end of the
tyranny – Alexander was succeeded by his wife's brothers Lycophron
and Tisiphonus, the children of Jason (Xen. *Hell.* 6.4.35–7).

   The unusual political makeup of Thessaly should not hinder our
understanding of the tyranny there. Jason created a long-lasting
and successful dynasty, although one which was not necessarily
recognised as such by his contemporaries – Aristotle, for instance,

omits Jason from his discussion of tyranny in the *Politics*, despite a passing reference to him as tyrant at *Pol.* 1277a 24–5. Jason is identifiable as an aristocrat aiming at sole power and finding both a quasi-constitutional form for doing so (like the *strategos autocrator* of Sicilian tyrannies) and significant opposition from other upper class groups. His use of mercenaries was innovative, but it was not the sole locus of his power; that was to be found in Thessaly at large and in Pherae in particular. But Jason's rule was neither old-fashioned nor backward-looking: his tyranny made Thessaly prosperous and influential, fully exploiting its manpower and resources to engage fully in Greek power politics.

The Hecatomnids of Caria

Our third ruler seems to take us a long way from classical tyranny: Mausolus of Halicarnassus, who ruled in Caria at the opposite end of the Greek world from the Dionysii between the 390s and 353, was another man of energy and vision. He inherited power from his father Hecatomnus, the Persian-appointed *satrap* of Caria, who was in constitutional terms a governor under the Persian king (Diod. 14.98.3). The fact that Mausolus inherited the rule from his father, however, shows that the *satrapy* was more than simply an administrative post. The Persians sought continuity of rulership in the countries of their empire, and were generally happy for their governors to hand on the role within the family; we see *satrapies* which pass from father or mother to son, from sister to brother, and even from husband to wife. As *satraps* were often originally chosen because they were the most prominent members of a community, many already held positions of power within their region independent of the Persian appointment, and this seems to have been true of the Hecatomnids. They were a family of long-standing importance in Caria; a man with a name indicating his

link to the family (Pixodarus son of Mausolus) had appeared as a
leader in the Ionian Revolt in the previous century (Hdt. 5.118.2).
Hecatomnus had made his mark on the country by building temples,
chiefly at the capital Mylasa, and when Mausolus, together with
his sister and wife Artemisia II, succeeded his father in 377/6 he
too proved to be more than a Persian caretaker. He immediately
embarked on a much greater project, moving his capital from
Mylasa to Halicarnassus on the coast and building a magnificent
new city there: it was provided with fortification walls and harbours,
including the 'secret harbour' used by Artemisia to such good effect
against the Rhodians (p.1), temples and a theatre, and a huge palace
for Mausolus himself (Diod. 15.90.2–3, Vitruv. De arch. 2.8.13). It
was a self-consciously Greek city, echoed on a smaller scale in a
series of walled cities up and down the coast. The move of centre
was prompted by a new direction in foreign policy: Mausolus saw
Caria's potential as a maritime power, and turned his attention to
the control of trade and the forming of alliances with the Greek
states among the Ionian islands. Capitalising on the discontent of
members of Athens' second naval empire he supported them in their
revolt of 357; in 355 he welcomed Rhodes, Chios, Byzantium and
Cos into alliance with Caria. Inland he brought the neighbouring
region of Lycia under his control, and ultimately created a sphere of
influence which reached from Erythrae in the north to Pisidia in the
south. Such empire-building was not really in keeping with his role
as satrap, and Mausolus took part in the Satraps' Revolt of 362, but
his rapid withdrawal suggests that he had no real aim of breaking
away from the Persian Empire; what he wanted was to be permitted
to follow his own ambitions under loose Persian command.[48]

Mausolus and Artemisia were philhellenes and were concerned,
like Dionysius, to make their names in Greece as well as at home,
establishing Halicarnassus as a cultural centre. Their most famous
project was of course the construction of the Mausoleum, a funeral

monument so opulent that it gave his name to the language. It was one of the seven wonders of the ancient world, combining elements of Greek temple and Egyptian pyramid with sculptural friezes and statues, and attracted the foremost artists of the day to work on it. Although the building itself is lost, it is described by the Roman writer Pliny (*NH* 36.30–1): on a stepped base, surrounded by friezes, stood a temple with thirty-six columns; on top of this was a twenty-four-step pyramid, equal in height to the building below, finishing in a platform carrying a statue of a four-horse chariot. The whole monument was a hundred and forty feet high. Such a construction was a long time in the building – it was begun under Mausolus, continued by Artemisia and finished after her death – and also hugely expensive, as indeed were the other civic and military projects. Large amounts of revenue were needed to pay for such grandiose policies, and while Mausolus' role as *satrap* involved the extraction of taxes for Persia, he also needed to raise his own revenues, and the *Oikonomika* describes some of his more ingenious methods: taxing corpses as they passed through the city gates and threatening to make his subjects shave their heads so that he could send their hair to the King, unless they bribed him to save their coiffures (Arist. *Oik.* 1348a 18–34).

Although the Hecatomnids were keen to align themselves with the Greek states, their rule preserved one very distinctively Carian feature: the right of women to hold power. Artemisia is in a tradition of powerful female rulers from Asia Minor stretching back to her namesake Artemisia I of Halicarnassus in the 480s: she was not a queen, but co-ruler with her brother, and after his death in 353 governed alone for a further two years (Diod. 16.36.2). Vitruvius celebrates her courage and dynamism in war with the conquest of Rhodes, but she attracted particular Greek ire: in 351 Demosthenes proposed helping the islanders of Rhodes to free themselves from Hecatomnid rule, and encouraged his audience thus: 'Would it not be disgraceful, my countrymen, if ... you who are Athenians should be frightened of a barbarian, and a woman at that!' (Dem. 15. 23). On her death her younger brother Idreius and sister Ada became rulers, and Hecatomnid rule continued until the conquests of Alexander in the late 330s.

One can ask whether Mausolus and Artemisia saw themselves (and whether we should recognise them) as tyrants, but confusion over their titles suggests that the question may have been as difficult to answer in antiquity as it is now. That Mausolus was more than a regular *satrap* is indicated by Diodorus, who makes a clear distinction between Ariobarzanes, Orontes and Autophradates, *satraps* of Phrygia, Mysia and Lydia respectively, and Mausolus, *dynastes* of Caria. (15.90.3) Their preferred title may have been *dynastes*, but a contemporary inscription and the near-contemporary *Oikonomika* refer to them as tyrants, while an Attic comedy of the period calls Mausolus 'king of the Carians'. The Hecatomnids may have had a hereditary religious role as 'kings', and if a *satrapy* is hereditary, as this appears to have been, then the difference between this and kingship in practice was slight.[49] But in their personal power – the ability to build cities, transplant populations, compel financial contributions and rule according to their will – and in their ambitions Mausolus and Artemisia stand with the tyrants of the age.

Tyranny in mainland Greece

We have seen so far three rulers representing different facets of autocratic power – the usurper, the mercenary leader and the *satrap* – and from these examples it is plain that asking whether such individuals were 'really' tyrants is not a particularly fruitful approach. The tyrants of the archaic age were easily categorised: supporters of the *demos* who seized unconstitutional power; wealthy men who made laws, beautified their cities and fostered the growth of the state. But definitions like this were the product of historians looking back over several generations when it was easy to fit all tyrants into a set pattern. When writing contemporary history it is much more difficult to impose a pattern on events and individuals: historians writing about events which they were living through were much less sure of the titles to give to the forms of government they saw. We have to ask what a contemporary would have made of a ruler like Pisistratus: would he have seemed very different to a Jason when he gathered his mercenaries and marched on Athens? The trade of mercenary had always existed in Greece – there are grafitti scratched by sixth-century Greek mercenaries on the statue of Rameses II at Abu Simbel[50] – and many archaic tyrants used mercenary forces in their rise to power. Would Histiaeus have seemed very different to Mausolus, or Artemisia I to her descendant? Class is also a factor: archaic tyrants are generally presented as champions of the *demos* against the aristocracy, and historians, being drawn from the upper classes, would naturally find the reality of a rabble-rousing leader disturbing.

Because our sources are closer to the men and women concerned, we can see the competition to control opinion: 'tyrant' was by this stage an emotive word, and formed part of the struggle to define a ruler's title. All of the individuals we have looked at were referred to in their own time as tyrants, yet each chose a title for himself to be used in official documents – *archon* for Dionysius, *tagos* for Jason and *dynastes* for Mausolus – which deliberately avoided the term. But this too is an issue of historical perspective. If we had contemporary sources for archaic tyrants we would not necessarily find them describing themselves as '*tyrannos*' either. Pittacus, for instance, though apparently elected to the role of *aisymnetes*, was abused as a tyrant by Alcaeus, and the Deinomenids chose to style themselves only as 'son of Deinomenes' in their dedications at

Olympia and Delphi.[51] It is therefore not surprising that contemporary historians often reflect fierce debates over the precise title to be given to certain leaders.

The case of Euphron, tyrant in Sicyon between 368 and 366, illustrates this particularly well. Euphron originally came to power with the aid of the Argives and Arcadians who were hoping to detach Sicyon from its alliance with Sparta and bring it over to the Theban axis. On entering the city he called an assembly and, with an Argive and Arcadian army standing by, declared that the constitution was to change to a democracy. He was elected general along with four others, and then gradually took control of affairs, banishing former pro-Spartans and putting his son in command of the mercenaries; according to Xenophon he 'was quite plainly a tyrant' (*Hell.* 7.1.44–6). Some time later he was overthrown by his former Arcadian allies and forced to flee; a civil war ensued, Euphron reappeared with a new mercenary army raised with money from Athens, and fought his way back into power. He again took the city and gained the support of the *demos*, but was unable to recapture the acropolis which had fallen into Theban hands. So he went to Thebes to negotiate an agreement, where he was assassinated by enemies who had followed him there (Xen. *Hell.* 7.3.1–12). The story is complex, but Xenophon leaves his readers in no doubt about what was going on: Euphron was, he says, by any definition a tyrant – he exiled men and confiscated their property, killed people without trial, freed slaves and stole temple treasures, and was justly murdered.

Xenophon paints Euphron as a pure opportunist, out to secure wealth and power for himself and his family and using powerful friends to do so, but there is reason to think that he had more personal and idealistic motives. As his first act he had established a democratic constitution, and after his death he was honoured by the citizens (including the newly enfranchised slaves) with heroic worship as the founder of the state. His opponents are characterised as the *plousiôtatoi* (richest), *beltistoi* (aristocracy) and *kratistoi* (most powerful), and one can read the conflict not as one of oppressive tyrant versus liberators, but as a familiar contest between rich and poor. This fits with the context of the 370s and 360s, and it is attractive to understand Euphron as leader of the democratic party, hoping to achieve not personal power alone, but a constitution which would favour the *demos*. This would explain his popularity among the citizens, which seems at odds with Xenophon's description of his crimes, and the support he received from democratic Athens: an Athenian inscription from 318/17 records a grant of citizenship to Euphron II, grandson of the tyrant, and his child, hinting at a long-standing connection with the family (*IG* ii² 448 (= Schwenk 83)). No doubt Euphron would have seen himself as champion of the *demos* and architect of a constitution 'on fair and equal terms': the citizens' posthumous honours for him suggest that they too saw him as 'refounding' the *polis* under a new constitution. The aristocrats, however, finding these acts hostile to their interests, could easily represent him as a lawless and self-serving usurper. A nobleman himself, Xenophon assesses Euphron from the point of view of the wealthy, making the very worst of his actions: using the resources of the state to prosecute foreign wars becomes temple robbery, and the enfranchisement of slaves an attack on fundamental social values. He implies that Euphron collected a mercenary force in order to enforce his rule on an unwilling city, but it is clear that he took over an existing army from the previous regime, and used it not to oppress his fellow citizens but to fight external wars. Euphron may have looked to stronger *poleis* for support, but he had a long-term project and aim, and was using the Arcadians and Athenians to achieve this, as much as being used by them.

Euphron also illustrates the part played by the growing habit of more powerful states of interfering in the political affairs of their neighbours. The political landscape of Greece had changed after the Peloponnesian War: our sources describe the years after 400 as an era of social instability resulting from the impoverishment of the states. All classes became poorer, but the least wealthy were of course the hardest hit, and many were made destitute. Competition between rich and poor to control resources therefore intensified, and the picture our sources present is one of *poleis* in turmoil, with constant *stasis* (civil war) leading to one or other side being exiled, just as happened at Sicyon. The exiles then formed a disaffected group outside the city, looking for an opportunity to return, and when they did, continued the cycle with exilings and confiscations of their own. Of course tyrants had been assisted into power by each other previously, and some of the old-style pattern could still be found: Dionysius I, for instance, encouraged a certain Aeimnestus to take power as tyrant at Enna in 403 (Diod. 14.14.6). But this was something different – states which were not themselves tyrannical encouraging tyrannies elsewhere because they made the allegiance of that city secure.

Significant in this connection are a less well-known group of rulers – the tyrants of Euboea. Events in Euboea between 366 and 346 are so fiendishly complicated that a narrative would hardly be welcome: suffice it to say that we hear of a discontinuous and rather confused series of tyrants. Themison ruled at Eretria in 366 in alliance with Thebes; Hipparchus ruled at Eretria and Philistides at Oreus, both established by Philip of Macedon in 348; in 346 Callias was in power at Chalcis in alliance with Athens.[52] Because the events concerned are so complex the episode is little discussed, yet it is of vital importance for our project – if tyrants were appearing just across the straits from Athens, and impinging on the Athenian sphere of influence so close to home, it gives a much sharper point to the discussions of tyranny in the fourth century. The immediacy

of events in Euboea makes it easy to understand the context of the
law of Eukrates against tyranny passed in Athens in 337/6.[53] The
law repeated earlier anti-tyranny legislation:

> If anyone rises up against the *Demos* to establish a tyranny, or
> joins in setting up a tyranny, or if anyone overthrows the *Demos*
> of Athens or the democracy at Athens, whoever kills the man
> who has done this shall be immune from prosecution.
>
> (ll. 7–11)

and added that if the constitution should be overthrown, it was
not permitted for the Councillors of the Areopagus to gather or
deliberate, on pain of loss of citizenship. This law was passed at a
time of great political anxiety for the Greeks, after their cataclysmic
battle against Philip at Chaeronea in August 338, which had left
Philip the effective ruler of Greece. It had been Philip's habit in the
past to assist in the establishment of friendly governments in Greek
states, and Demosthenes represented him as both a tyrant himself
and a friend to tyranny in general. There is in fact little sign that
Philip spent much time pondering the merits of different constitutional forms, being a man of action rather than thought, but he
was quite prepared to favour any kind of rule which allowed him
to exert a direct influence on the policy of a state; he encouraged
tyrannies at Megara and Messene at the same time as overthrowing
Lycophron and Peitholaus, the successors of Alexander of Pherae, in
Thessaly (Diod. 16.38.1). The Athenians obviously feared that in the
aftermath of defeat a tyrant might be imposed on them, and that
the Areopagus Council might agree to sanction his rule, especially
in the light of the disastrous management of the war against
Macedon by the democratic government. Although a tyranny did
not in fact emerge at this stage, under the Successors of Alexander
the Athenians were to receive exactly this kind of ruler, as we shall
see in the next chapter.

Conclusion

The law of Eukrates demonstrates how politically charged the idea of tyranny had become by the fourth century. The term 'tyrant' was widely applied as a political insult: at Thebes, for instance, a revolution took place in 387, brought about by the Spartan general Phoebidas, and an oligarchic junta took charge. These men were not tyrants as such, but both Xenophon and Plutarch use the term to describe them, and likewise the name 'Thirty Tyrants' was applied to the group who held power at Athens from 404 to 401. It is thus not surprising that some rulers sought to dissociate themselves from the concept of tyranny, but there is clearly little that is new about the nature of their rule. The problems of the *polis* – *stasis*, external threat, political divisiveness – had not changed, and tyrants were actually well positioned to prosper in the fourth century. They could, for instance, take control of finances: the impoverished Greek states found it hard to take the necessary measures to reestablish their prosperity, and a tyrant had the power to set long-term policy, and to compel contributions. Personal leadership was another issue, of which Jason is a good example – he had the vision to pull the cities of Thessaly together and exploit its manpower and resources, and while he lived it was a successful strategy. We may compare events in Thebes in the 370s and 60s under Epaminondas, another visionary leader who brought about Theban domination first of Boiotia and then the Peloponnese, but who suffered from internal opposition – enmity from political rivals led to his being deposed and indicted on several occasions, and made continuity of policy much harder to ensure. At a time when smaller states were coming under increasing pressure from their larger neighbours, a tyrant could also unite the city behind a charismatic man who could act as general in a time of threat, and represented the city's interest, as at Euboea.[54]

Because our sources for the fourth century are closer to the period they describe we are better able to see the competing claims of pro- and anti-tyrannical traditions: we have both detailed analysis of the moral and political failings of rulers, and the very different propaganda of the tyrants themselves. Tyranny was a topic about which Greek writers found it hard to be consistent; the Greeks said they were against tyranny, and said it more vociferously as the century went on, yet at the same time came to recognise its advantages. We have already seen Demosthenes' gloomy comparison of Philip's dynamism with democratic Athens' difficulty in forming and carrying out policy, and the next chapter will examine these divided attitudes in more detail, in order to discover their roots.

CHAPTER 4

PHILOSOPHERS AND
TYRANTS

A further story of Dionysius I concerns his encounter with the philosopher Plato. Plato visited Syracuse around 388 BC and gained the friendship of Dion, brother-in law of the tyrant. Dion persuaded Dionysius to meet Plato and listen to his philosophical ideas, but the meeting was unfortunate: Plato in provocative mood declared that the life of a tyrant was by nature unhappy, and that only the just could attain virtue and happiness, which naturally roused Dionysius' anger. Plato then left Sicily, and Dionysius gave orders for him to be killed on the journey home, or to be seized and sold as a slave. 'It would do Plato no harm,' said the tyrant, 'since according to his own ideas, as a just man he should be able to be happy even if he were enslaved.' (Plut. *Dion* 5) Thus Plato found himself on the sale block in the slave market at Aegina, and was saved only at the intervention of his friends who purchased him and set him free again.

The story, most likely invented, illustrates the dangers of trying out philosophy on a tyrant, but also, more importantly, the close links which came to exist between tyranny and philosophy. Thinkers such as Plato, Aristotle and Isocrates devoted much of their time to discussions of methods of rule and of the virtues of the ruler, while tyrants for their part sought to attract philosophers to their courts as intellectual ornaments or as practical advisers. The advice of the philosopher was not always welcome, of course, but the rewards could be great: if their ideas proved popular, they could receive influential support from an interested patron, and could potentially influence a ruler's style or methods of government. Tyrants were particularly attractive to philosophers because of the unbounded power which they enjoyed: a tyrant could, if he were a man of sufficient wisdom and virtue, adopt philosophical principles and legislate to create an ideal *polis*, at least in theory. So Aristotle spent time at the court of Hermias of Atarneus, and Plato made several visits to Syracuse.

Philosophy was, in fourth-century Athens, not a widespread activity: it was an upper-class pursuit, for those whose fathers could afford to support them in idleness as they spent days listening to lectures and discussing ideas. The young men of Plato's circle were universally wealthy and aristocratic, and philosophers tended in general to be unsympathetic to the idea of democracy. As a result, considerable hostility was directed towards philosophers, including Plato, on the grounds that they were pro-tyrannical: that they courted the favour of existing tyrants and encouraged the wealthy young men whom they taught to aspire to tyranny themselves (Athenaeus *Deipn.* 504a–9d). This chapter will look at the connections between three influential philosophers – Plato, Aristotle and Isocrates – and tyranny, and consider the accuracy of these accusations.

Plato and the philosopher-king

Plato is best known for his *Republic*, a blueprint for the ideal state which takes the form of a discussion between Socrates and his friends in which Socrates explains how the city could best be organised to produce a virtuous and enlightened community. Every aspect of civic life is covered, from education and family life to military and political organisation, and Plato's work includes some alarming and radical suggestions, such as the idea that women should hold public office (5.454–6) and exercise naked with men (5.457), and that children should be raised communally instead of in families (5.461). Fundamental to the plan was the idea that philosophers, as the only people truly qualified for rulership, should govern the state, and Plato argues this at length: Socrates suggests that only a man truly dedicated to moral virtue was capable of bringing the state to the same condition, and proposes that a small group of morally and intellectually superior people should rule the rest (5.473). Because of their personal goodness they would not seek personal gain, but would benefit all.

Proposing such an idea, however, made it appear that Plato and his circle were advocating tyranny, with one ruler above the law, and consequently Plato was careful to distinguish between this type of monarchy on the one hand, which was desirable, and tyranny on the other, which was not. Book VIII of the *Republic* surveys the four types of 'false' constitution: the timarchic, like that of Crete and Sparta, oligarchy, democracy and tyranny, and tyranny is described as the worst disorder a state can suffer. Socrates suggests that the state naturally declines from best to worst, so tyranny, by this argument, is the nadir of constitutions, developing from an extreme of democracy. The tyrant begins as a champion of the poor, liberating debtors and redistributing land, he stirs up war and impoverishes his subjects, becomes unpopular, then begins on purges, frees slaves and confiscates sacred treasures (9.571–80). The discussion ends with a comparison between the best constitution (the royal) and the worst (the tyrannical) designed to show that however attractive the life of a tyrant might appear, he is in fact the prisoner of fear and paranoia, friendless, faithless and tormented by unfulfilled desire. Only the just man who pursues honour and virtue can know happiness, and Socrates calculates that the king is 729 times happier than the tyrant (9.587).

The calculation on this point may seem unconvincing, and indeed the argument too, but the unattractive nature of tyranny was a surprisingly frequent topic among philosophers. It appears several times in Plato (*Rep.* 619b-d, *Gorgias* 469c–71d), while Xenophon devoted a whole work, the *Hieron*, to the theme, a sure sign that it was a topic of wider interest. Xenophon was not a major philosophical thinker, but a man of wide literary interests who picked up on and popularised the ideas of more radical figures. His *Oikonomikos*, for instance, gives a watered-down form of Aristotle and Plato's ideas on the correct organisation of the household: Plato argued that men and women should be treated equally, according to their individual talents, but in Xenophon's work the idea is presented in the less radical form that women have their own areas of competence (primarily domestic work and childcare) and so the running of the household should be a joint venture between husband and wife, each in their own sphere. In the same way the *Hieron* takes philosophical ideas about the tyrant and presents them in a simpler form. It takes the form of a historical dialogue between Hieron I, tyrant of Syracuse, and the poet Simonides, in which Simonides suggests that the life of a tyrant is the most enviable possible, with constant praise, luxurious feasts, beautiful women and the best of everything, while Hieron demonstrates in answer to each point that the tyrant is in fact most unhappy: he cannot trust his friends or family, is jaded in his appetites and can take no pleasure in the luxury which surrounds him. The theme surfaces in other stories such as that of Damon and Pythias: there is always a tyrant in the story who initially intends to kill one of the friends, but who ends up so awed by the devotion they show to each other that he pardons them and asks to become their friend himself. Why so much emphasis on the misery of the tyrant's lot? The answer is simple: because in the popular imagination being a tyrant was clearly the best which life had to offer: wealth, luxury, power and self-indulgence.[55] Philosophers, in claiming that tyranny was in fact miserable, were setting up a deliberately contradictory idea, aiming both to elevate their own intellectual preoccupations over worldly ones, and to avoid accusations of advocating autocratic rule. Hence the concern to belittle the delights of tyrant life and the character of those who would seek it.

For all his condemnation of tyranny as the worst form of constitution, Plato found himself turning back to it when faced with the question of how the ideal state could be brought into being. The *Republic* imagined a situation where a state fell under the control of one or more benevolent and philosophically minded rulers who had the power to legislate as they wished, and the ability to enforce compliance from the citizens. Adults above the age of ten would then be relegated to the countryside and the children could be brought up under the new regime to form the first generation of new citizens (*Rep.* 5.450–1). The concept is a dramatic and chilling one, but Plato's view of the necessity of autocracy is striking: only extraordinary political power could bring about the revolution. In his *Statesman* some years later he made an explicit statement that the rule of a man who understands true statesmanship would be better than any existing constitution, because only the statesman could rule with true political expertise and understanding (293–4). Later on in the *Laws* – an attempt to draw up a practical lawcode for a newly founded city – Plato retreated from the idea of the philosopher-king, proposing instead that the city be ruled by a small group of morally excellent magistrates, but still retained the reliance on tyranny to produce change (*Laws* 709e–11e).[56]

Plato's *Republic* and *Laws* were theoretical exercises, but there was at least the potential to apply the ideas in practice. This turns on the evidence of Plato's *Seventh Letter*, an intriguing document discussing his involvement with the Dionysii in Syracuse. The *Letter* is addressed from Plato to the relatives and friends of Dion, and gives a detailed account of Plato's three visits to Syracuse between

388 and 360, and the reasons for his actions. There is a long-standing debate over whether the letter is genuine or whether it was written by Plato's supporters after his death in order to justify his actions to his detractors, but even if the *Letter* was written later, the events and ideas it describes are still substantially accurate.[57] After his first disastrous visit and brush with the slave-traders, Plato was invited to return to give Dionysius' successor Dionysius II the benefit of his philosophy. In the *Letter* Plato gives his reasons for acceding to Dion's request, and they echo very strongly the ideas of the *Republic* and *Laws*: 'if ever one were going to put into practice these ideas about laws and government, now was the time to try; for if I could persuade just one man, I would be able to achieve complete success' (328c). Nevertheless the author of the *Letter* betrays a striking unease at the idea of fraternising with a tyrant: Plato emphasises that he did not approve of tyranny, and that his motives for attending the court were entirely high-minded, namely his obligations to Dion and his concern to bring the philosophical life to the citizens of Syracuse. Unfortunately Dionysius II was no more to be influenced than his father: although he was initially very taken with Plato and his ideas, and even went so far as to criticise the institution of tyranny, Plato was only one of a number of rival thinkers at the court, all competing for the tyrant's attention and favour, and the initial appeal of his rather austere teachings soon faded. Dion was exiled on suspicion of conspiracy and Plato was apparently detained for a time by the tyrant before he returned to Athens (329b–330b). But it is interesting that Plato (or his followers) could credit the idea of influencing a ruler to introduce Platonic legislation.

Plato's friendship with the tyrant's brother-in-law Dion, even more than with the Dionysii, was problematic because it raised the question of just how close the links between philosopher and tyrant could become. The story of Dion is most interesting for the light it casts on questions of interpretation. Dion is presented in our sources unequivocally as a hero, a liberator who brought freedom to Syracuse, ending the tyranny out of committed principle. Plutarch chose to pair his biography with that of Brutus, assassin of Julius Caesar. This is certainly one way of reading the story: Dion was converted to the philosophy of Plato early on, and was responsible for the attempt to introduce Plato to Dionysius II's court, hoping to influence the tyrant into adopting philosophical principles of rule. Dion himself is described as the opposite of the self-indulgent tyrant, a severe and self-disciplined man who rejected any form of luxury or vice in favour of a life of service and philosophical discussion. Plutarch depicts him as a lone virtuous figure at the Syracusan court, disliked by the tyrant's other advisors and ultimately the subject of a plot to undermine his position. In a plot led by Philistus a letter was given to Dionysius apparently revealing that Dion was conspiring with the Carthaginians to gain power. Dion was exiled in 366 and went to Athens; his property was confiscated by Dionysius, and his wife Arete forced to remarry a friend of the tyrant (Plut. *Dion* 18–21). Dion spent his exile at the Academy in Athens as part of Plato's circle, and at first tried through Plato to be reconciled with Dionysius, but finally he determined to return to Syracuse at the head of an army, and try to overthrow the tyranny. He recruited both Syracusan exiles and mercenary soldiers, and sailed back to Sicily in 357 at the head of a tiny army. Dion and his men landed at the port of Minoa where he gathered armour and supplies, and from there advanced on Syracuse, gathering support from the surrounding cities as he went. At Syracuse Dionysius happened to be away, and the 'invasion' met with an enthusiastic response: the citizens opened the gates to Dion and welcomed him, while the tyrant's supporters fled. Dion proclaimed the city free of the tyranny, and he and his brother Megacles were immediately elected *strategoi autocratores*, with a council of twenty others to assist in government (Diod. 16.9–10, Plut. *Dion* 29.4).

The triumphant liberation, however, was only the beginning of events. The citadel at Ortygia had remained in the hands of Dionysius' bodyguards, and a week later the tyrant returned to Syracuse. Although he was unable to recapture the city, he was able to remain in his palace, which was impregnable, and he entered into negotiations with Dion and the Syracusans, suggesting that he might surrender on favourable terms. At this stage Dion began to encounter opposition, as he was accused of favouring Dionysius because of their family connection, and of aiming to take the tyranny for himself rather than abolishing it. Dionysius retired to Italy, leaving his soldiers to hold Ortygia. Other more populist leaders led a campaign against Dion, and he was forced to retire with his mercenaries to Leontini. Seizing the opportunity, Dionysius sent his admiral with a fleet to support his soldiers, and they launched a surprise night attack on the Syracusans in the city. The city was thrown into confusion and great slaughter ensued; the panicking Syracusans sent to Dion and begged him to bring his army back and protect them. Dion immediately did so, won a swift victory and was once again hailed by the people:

> Once the assembly was summoned, the *demos* in gratitude elected Dion *strategos autocrator* and awarded him honours appropriate for a hero, and Dion in accordance with his previous conduct generously cleared all his opponents of the charges against them, and with gentle words brought the people to general harmony. And the Syracusans unanimously praised and honoured him as their benefactor and sole saviour of their country.
>
> (Diod. 16.20.6)

The tyrant's son Apollocrates handed over the citadel and sailed away, and Dion was reunited with his wife and family.

This is the story as told in outline by Diodorus, emphasising the nobility of Dion's character and the purity of his motives. He succeeded in bringing freedom to the Syracusans, and was rewarded by a grateful populace. Yet certain episodes indicate that there is another way of interpreting events. Take Dion's original exile, on a suspicion of plotting against the tyranny with Carthage. Our sources say that Dion was unpopular at court because of his unbending virtue, and hence became the subject of plots, yet when he led his army to Sicily he ended up at Minoa, a town under Carthaginian control, where the governor happened to be a friend of his (Plut. *Dion* 25.11–14). This friend, Synalos, was able to supply Dion with the armour and stores he required, which might make us think again about the initial accusations. Dion's stated aim was to liberate the Syracusans from tyranny, yet on his entry to the city he was elected to the position of *strategos autocrator*, the same as that held by the tyrants; one might see a disaffected member of the tyranny's inner circle raising an army of mercenaries in order to seize power for himself. The most telling episode is the aftermath of the liberation, when the Syracusans attempted to find a new constitution under which to govern themselves. Dion, true to his philosophical principles, proposed to establish a new constitution, not a democracy which as a Platonist he disdained, but a 'blend of democracy and monarchy on the Spartan or Cretan model' (Plut. *Dion* 53.4), which we have seen was Plato's best constitution. This undoubtedly meant a highly controlled state with a king or kings and a council of elders, and was not what the Syracusans had expected of liberation. Other democratic leaders had emerged to rival Dion, notably Heracleides, and they did not support the idea of a narrow oligarchic constitution. Dion therefore found himself not the undisputed leader of a grateful and malleable city, but one of a number of political rivals, and soon he abandoned his high principles and had Hercleides murdered (Plut. *Dion* 53.5–6). Plutarch and Diodorus do what they can to exonerate Dion from blame, suggesting that he was persuaded to the murder by his friends, and that Heracleides deserved to die, but it is nevertheless true that Dion was becoming the kind of leader that he had criticised so strongly. Another rival, Callippus the Athenian, started a rumour that Dion intended to make Apollocrates, son of Dionysius II and Dion's own nephew, his political heir and to reinstate the tyranny, and in 354 Dion was himself assassinated (Plut. *Dion* 57, Diod. 16.31.7). Callippus went on to become tyrant for a short time, before he was in turn replaced by Hipparinus, brother of Dionysius II; Dion's overthrow of the tyranny had not lasted long.

Considered from one perspective, then, Dion was a philosophically minded liberator who brought freedom to Syracuse, but whose motives were fatally misunderstood: from another he was a member of a tyrannical family who raised a mercenary army and sought to gain power for himself by force. The reasons he has been remembered so favourably are two: the fact that he died so soon after taking power, before his new constitution and motives were really put to the test, and the concern of successive leaders of the Academy to protect Plato's reputation – Dion's exploits had done nothing to deflect the accusations of training young men to become tyrants, and the *Seventh Letter* was composed to present Plato's defence.

Aristotle

Aristotle's aim was the same as Plato's: to identify and describe the best constitutional form for the *polis*. His *Politics* is in a less complete state than the *Republic* and *Laws* but its arguments are still plain: Aristotle's preferred constitution was what he calls '*politeia*', described as a mixed constitution sharing the characteristics of democracy and oligarchy, and he begins to formulate the system in the later books of the work. But the process by which he arrived at this conclusion was different from Plato. Aristotle was not writing from a purely abstract perspective, deciding principles of good government first and then creating the plan to achieve them. Instead his technique was a scientific one, gathering evidence and then using it to develop an overall theory. He applied this principle extensively to natural phenomena such as animals, plants and weather events, and to more abstract areas too, including forms of governments. As outlined above, he sent his pupils around the Mediterranean to collect information from as many cities as they could, about their constitutional forms and histories, and created a collection of 158 different constitutions. Only one has survived virtually complete, that of Athens which was discovered on a papyrus in 1890, although the *Politics* contains significant material from certain others, such as Carthage and Crete. Using these constitutions as his material, Aristotle wrote the *Politics* aiming to classify all existing constitutions within a single system, and to explain how they came into being or were destroyed. Even though his ultimate goal was to identify the best constitution, he devoted extensive discussion to all contemporary forms. He was particularly interested, in the light of the unrest he saw in the *poleis* around him, in the reasons for the failure of constitutions, and to draw from this prescriptions for their preservation. An analysis of tyranny was thus part of his project, and, as we have seen, this is one of the most important sources for ancient tyrants and extremely influential on modern understanding of the phenomenon.

Just like Plato, Aristotle saw tyranny as a bad form of government, contrary to the rule of law and contrasting with monarchy which had all the good characteristics. Indeed Aristotle could be said to have invented tyranny by setting out typical tyrannical forms and actions drawn from historical examples. In general he depicts tyrants as hostile to their people, cutting off the aristocrats and oppressing the poor, attacking and insulting women and men and so calling down vengeance on themselves, and constantly in fear of attack. He says that there are two possible strategies by which a tyrant can preserve his rule: he can secure his position by oppression, removing any rivals ruthlessly, disarming the population and spying on them to prevent conspiracies, or he can rule in an enlightened way, converting the tyranny to something more like a monarchy by exerting himself for the general good. The ruler should cultivate self-control, help the city to prosper, be religiously circumspect and adorn the city. He should get either the people or the nobles onto his side, and so avoid the necessity for freeing slaves and confiscation of arms (*Pol.* 1314a 29–1315b 11). In this way the difference between the tyrant and the monarch seems moral rather than constitutional.

Definition in fact proved difficult, as noted in the introduction, because it was possible to find sole rulers who were elected, not kings but not tyrants either. Rulers such as Pittacus, who held the position of *aisymnetes*, or the kings of Thrace occupied a grey area between the two, and Aristotle categorises them differently at different points.[58] The difficulty of drawing clear demarcations is further illustrated by the examples used in the discussion of tyrants. Some seem to fit the bill very easily – Pisistratus, Periander, Dionysius II – but others sit less comfortably – the Persian kings, for instance, Sardanapalus and Cotys of Thrace (*Pol.* 1311b 20–1312a 4). Most striking is the lack of contemporary examples in this analysis: only the Dionysii play a major role as tyrannical exemplars, while figures like Jason and Alexander of Pherae, Euphron of Sicyon and Clearchus of Heracleia are conspicuous by their absence, although Jason is mentioned once in an earlier section of the book (1277a 24–5). Nowhere is this more surprising that at section 1315 where Aristotle asserts that tyrannies are usually of short duration. He names as the three longest-lasting dynasties the Orthagorids at Sicyon (which lasted for a hundred years), the Cypselids at Corinth (seventy-three and a half years) and the Pisistratids at Athens (thirty-five years). Apart from these, he says, and the eighteen-year rule of the Deinomenids in Syracuse, no tyranny has lasted a significant length of time. All four of his examples date to the sixth or early fifth century, yet some of the longest tyrannies existed in Aristotle's own time. The Dionysii, who together ruled for forty-nine years, should certainly make the list, as should Jason and his successors at Pherae with a combined rule of about thirty years; Clearchus and his sons are not mentioned at all. I suspect that this is because Aristotle's definition of tyranny (a usurper who is oppressive and paranoid and whose rule cannot last long) was based on earlier examples and so fits contemporary rulers less well.

Aristotle was hostile to tyranny in print, seeing tyrants as given to *hubris* and paranoia, yet in reality he was more tolerant. He might not have found the opportunity to put his ideal constitution into practice, but he had connections with two tyrants who did. *Pol.* 1296a states that mixed constitutions have to date been rare, and only one lawgiver allowed a *politeia*. The lawgiver concerned is not named, but it has been suggested that it may refer to Aristotle's friend, Hermias of Atarneus. Hermias was a Greek tyrant who came to rule in Atarnaeus in Mysia in the late 350s, and created a little kingdom there within Persian territory. He had previously studied at Plato's Academy in Athens and once established in power he invited some of the Platonists to set up a school in his territory at Assos. Aristotle was among those who settled there, marrying Hermias' niece and evidently influencing his style of government, which became 'a milder form of rule'. It is not known how far Aristotle was able to go in persuading Hermias to implement his political theories, but the association was to rebound rather dramatically on him when Hermias was discovered to have been intriguing with Philip of Macedon against Persia. Hermias was arrested and tortured, and since Aristotle had by this stage moved to Macedon to take up the position of tutor to the young Alexander, suspicions of pro-Macedonian conspiracy were felt to be justified. Aristotle later

wrote an encomium of Hermias which attracted much criticism on
the grounds of both blasphemy and friendship with tyrants.[59]

Aristotelian influence was also felt in Athens in the 320s. After
the death of Alexander the Great his generals fought for possession
of Greece, and Athens was captured by the Macedonians more than
once, first by Antipater in 322, and then by Cassander in 317. The
Macedonian conquerors left a garrison in Athens to assure the co-
operation of the citizens, and showed no hesitation in altering the
constitution. In 322 Antipater introduced a property qualification
for citizenship of 2,000 *drachmai*, limiting political rights to about
a third of the citizens and thus putting an end to the famous
democracy. When Cassander took over he chose to control the
city even more closely by occupying Munychia and appointing an
'overseer' (*epimeletes*) to administer the city. The man he chose was
Demetrius of Phaleron, a pupil of Theophrastus at the Lycaeum, and
under Macedonian auspices Demetrius held power in Athens for ten
years between 317 and 307 (Diod. 18.74.3). The nature of his rule
is much debated; opinions were divided even in his own time. His
position as *epimeletes* is not in doubt, but Plutarch says that under
him Athens was nominally an oligarchy, though in fact a monarchy
owing to Demetrius' great influence, while Pausanias refers to him
as a tyrant.[60] The presence of the Macedonian garrison at Munychia
certainly meant that Demetrius, like a tyrant, had unlimited power,
and he used the opportunity to introduce a series of political
and social reforms along the lines suggested by Aristotle. Athens
was still an oligarchy, although the citizenship qualification had
been reduced from 2,000 to 1,000 *drachmai*, with magistrates and
councillors elected instead of being chosen by lot. The wealthy were
freed from the burden of paying liturgies for festivals and ships,
while the Theoric Fund, which paid for poor citizens to attend the
dramatic festivals, was abolished. Demetrius also introduced laws
to limit conspicuous consumption by the rich: women's dress, the

amount spent on entertainments, ostentatious funeral monuments and even the number of guests at parties. Groups of officials were appointed to enforce obedience to these laws – Athenaeus (*Deipn.* 6.245a) tells the story of one Chairophon who gatecrashed a wedding party and was lying on the last couch. When the *gynaikonomoi* arrived they counted the guests and told Chairophon to leave, as he was exceeding the limit of thirty guests. 'Count again,' Chairophon told them, 'and this time start with me!'

Undoubtedly Demetrius' reforms were beneficial to Athens: with no significant expenditure on military affairs he was able to put the city's finances back in order and was credited with regulating prices and ensuring justice. Yet the interpretation of the legislation is difficult: was he a pro-aristocratic tyrant or a practical philosopher-king? The question is complicated by the lurid stories about his private life which exist in the tradition alongside the sober legislation. Can we credit a philosopher-king who held luxurious dinners every day in rooms sprinkled with perfume and flowers, who had a giant mechanical snail to lead his processions, or who wore makeup and conducted affairs with women and young men (Polyb. 12.13, Athen. *Deipn.* 542b–543a)? Such stories may be inventions of hostile historians (though it would be a brave historian who would invent the mechanical snail), but the Athenians themselves seem to have been divided in their attitudes towards him: we are told that during Demetrius' ten-year rule he was awarded more than three hundred bronze statues by the populace, but when his power came to an end on Cassander's death these statues were pulled down, some thrown into the sea and some melted down and reused to make chamber pots (Diog. Laert. 5.77). This last is a common story about the statues of unpopular rulers, but should we see Demetrius as an unpopular Macedonian-imposed tyrant, or an enlightened and beneficial ruler? The truth, as ever, probably depended on one's social status: he aimed to give power to the wealthier classes at the expense of the poor, and no doubt a man who had lost the citizen rights he had held under the democracy, along with access to the Theoric Fund, found the prosperity enjoyed by his more fortunate fellow-citizens hard to swallow. Probably this is what the philosophers' ideal constitution might look like, although it is ironic that it needed a tyrannical ruler to prevent the *demos* from overthrowing it. However philosophical Demetrius' purposes, too, it is worth bearing in mind that his power was not assured by popular support: backed by the Macedonian soldiers at Munychia, he could legislate as he liked without fear of opposition. Demetrius neatly exposes the paradox of the ideal constitution which has to be imposed on people for their own good.

Isocrates

Isocrates, the third of our philosophers, was a rather different kind of thinker. He differs from Plato and Aristotle because his ideas were more practical, but had the same tendency in favour of one-man rule. Isocrates was by profession a teacher of rhetoric and attracted many famous and distinguished pupils; he did not produce an overall theory of political practice or a body of philosophical works, but engaged in a more direct way with the political realities of his time. An Athenian like Plato, Isocrates lived a very long life from before the Peloponnesian War to the battle of Chaeronea in 338, in the course of which he saw huge upheavals in the political life of Greece. He grew up in an era of defeat and decline: his family had lost their money in the Peloponnesian War, and he saw the failure of the Athenian Empire followed by years of inconclusive warfare as the Greek *poleis* fought for short-lived advantage. Isocrates was not a general or an orator – he says that his voice was too weak for him to be an effective speaker – but published a series of letters and addresses in which he proposed practical solutions to the current dire circumstances of Greece.

In his writings he sketches a picture of impoverishment and social breakdown among the Greek cities: because of the constant fighting there is lawlessness within the *poleis*, with men being killed or exiled, and outside the *polis* a mass of wandering mercenaries who endanger everyone. War leads to destitution which in turn creates more conflict. Isocrates' answer was radical, and reached back to the certainties of the past: the Greeks should unite against a common enemy, as they had done in 480 when Xerxes invaded, and setting aside their pointless struggles for power wage a new war against Persia. He was particularly distressed at the agreements made with Persia during and after the Peloponnesian War which had handed control of the Ionian *poleis* back to the King, seeing this as a betrayal of Hellenic solidarity. Instead of allowing Persia to rule Greek cities, he argued, the Greeks should split off a chunk of territory from the Persian empire, from Sinope in the north to Cilicia in the south, and settle it with landless Greeks:

> It is open to a man who is high-minded and patriotic, and who possesses greater vision than most, by using the services of these people against the barbarians, to divide off the region which I mentioned earlier, and to free those who serve in a foreign land from the misfortunes which they currently suffer, and from those which they inflict on others, and by settling them in cities there to create a boundary for Greece and set them before the rest of us as a safeguard.
>
> (Isocrates *Philippus* 122)

This is at one level the lament of a dispossessed aristocrat: the years between 430 and 380 had seen the rich lose their wealth while the poor became destitute, and Isocrates wanted a return to the old certainties, where the wealthy were not threatened by the poor. On another, though, it had the virtue of wholesale reform, promising a new wave of colonisation to provide for the destitute.[61]

Isocrates' first approach for a leader of his panhellenic expedition was to Athens in the *Panegyricus*, but he soon realised that traditionally ruled states such as Athens, Sparta and Thebes were not capable of uniting the Greeks in the way he intended and turned his attention to the tyrants. He addressed himself first to Jason of Pherae and then to Dionysius I, urging them to take over the leadership of Greece and begin the campaign, as Jason at least is supposed to have planned. In neither case was his persuasion successful – Jason was assassinated before his plans came to fruition, and Dionysius was concerned with Italy rather than Persia – but Isocrates did not give up, and in 346 he saw another potential leader in Philip of Macedon. In the *Philippus*, the most complete statement of his plan, he encourages Philip to unite the Greeks and then take advantage of the weakness of the Persian Empire to conquer, if not the whole of the empire, then at least Asia Minor.

Isocrates was not unaware of the difficulty in writing to tyrants and kings, urging them to act for the good of Greece as a whole. Indeed he displays some ambivalence towards Dionysius, describing him in the *Philippus* as having 'a mad and unreasoning passion for monarchy' (65). But he was also aware that monarchy held considerable advantages for a project such as his. Early on in his career he wrote three orations for the kings of Salamis in Cyprus, Euagoras and Nicocles; the *Euagoras* is an encomium to the founder of the monarchy, but the two addressed to Nicocles are more in the vein of political advice, describing how a king should rule and how the subjects of a monarch should behave. Many of these ideas are similar to Aristotle's, suggesting that the king should rule mildly and with his subjects' good as his goal, but Isocrates has some more positive things to say about the advantages of monarchy. A monarch manages the state better, because he can reward excellence, provide continuity of rule (in contrast to fixed-term magistrates), and will value wisdom rather than rhetoric from his advisors. Kings are particularly favoured in military affairs because it is more efficient to appoint one man with full powers to run a campaign than to have many leaders. Isocrates advances Dionysius as an example of what a monarch could achieve in making Sicily the greatest of Hellenic states (*Phil.* 65, *Arch.* 44–5). Such comments, with their overt criticisms of democratic and oligarchic regimes, attracted hostility: in the *Antidosis* of 353 Isocrates had to make the point that he did not court Nicocles' favour for money or influence (40). Of course Isocrates proved to be prescient in the short term, because Philip and Alexander did in fact carry out the conquest of Persia, although Philip's motives for the Persia campaign were less high-minded, and his conquest of Greece not at all what Isocrates had in mind.

Clearchus of Heracleia: tyranny in practice

All three philosophers and their ideas come together in the figure of Clearchus of Heracleia, who stands at the intersection between philosophy, personal ambition and civil strife.[62] Clearchus established a tyranny at Heracleia on the Black Sea, a city founded around 560 by settlers from Megara and Boeotia and prosperous from the Black Sea trade routes. In the early fourth century Heracleia suffered some kind of *stasis* between democrats and oligarchs, as was common at that period. Clearchus was an aristocrat and supporter of the democratic faction; he had been exiled by the oligarchs for political opposition, and entered the employ of the neighbouring *satrap* Mithridates as a mercenary captain. In 364 *stasis* between the ruling oligarchic council and the *demos* had become acute, and the oligarchs decided to call in help to consolidate their position. Clearchus was the man they chose, and they invited him to return to the city as arbitrator of the civil disputes (Justin 16.4.1–4).

High-minded though this sounds, motives were bad on both sides: the council expected Clearchus to organise the city in their favour, while Clearchus saw an opportunity to extend personal power over the city. Gathering a mercenary army he entered Heracleia and occupied the city, launching a coup against the council and aligning himself firmly with the people. He was elected *strategos autocrator* at an emergency assembly. He took some of the councillors prisoner and the others fled, whereupon he confiscated their estates, freed their slaves and enfranchised them, and married off their wives and daughters to his supporters. Their property was redistributed among Clearchus' supporters, easing the economic problems of the poor, and with the support of the *demos* Clearchus established himself firmly as tyrant (Justin 16.4.10–5.6). He is most famous for the style in which he ruled, living on the acropolis, dressing as a stage king and declaring himself to be the son of Zeus. He maintained close relations with the Persian King and presided over a prosperous trade with Greece; his court became an intellectual centre, with one of the earliest libraries and a philosophical school run by a pupil of Plato.[63]

Clearchus was, however, an embarrassment to all three Athenian philosophers: as a wealthy exile he had travelled to Athens in the 370s to study first with Isocrates, taking his four-year course of study in rhetoric, and then briefly joining Plato's circle. When he made his coup in Heracleia, he laid the Athenian philosophers open to an accusation of training tyrants, and although he encouraged philosophers to settle in Heracleia his violence and radical reforms reflected badly on those seen as his mentors. Even Clearchus' death proved awkward for Plato, since the tyrant was assassinated by two young men, Chion and Leonides, both students from the Academy. Chion was the philosopher at Clearchus' court, and seems at one stage to have hoped to convert Clearchus into a philosopher-king, but finally to have despaired of the tyrant's rule. He and Leonides formed a conspiracy and stabbed Clearchus during a public festival, but were themselves killed by his bodyguard (Justin 16.5.12–18). Philosophy was thus seen to lead to violent deeds, either the creation of tyranny or its overthrow, making it a dangerous pastime for a city to encourage.

Clearchus is usually projected as a story of failure: a man who despite starting out as a philosopher became a bad tyrant and who met his end at the hands of more virtuous men. Yet the telling of the story in this way is the same kind of 'end-stopping' as in the archaic period, since Clearchus in fact established a very successful dynasty. After his death his brother Satyrus acted as regent for Clearchus' two sons and on Satyrus' death in 346 Timotheus became tyrant, with his brother Dionysius (named after the Syracusan) as co-ruler. After nine years Timotheus died, and Dionysius took over a powerful and prosperous Heracleia. He went from strength to strength, making a brilliant marriage to a Persian princess named Amastris, a niece of Darius III, and extending Heracleote control over the surrounding area. Shortly before his death he proclaimed himself king. On his death Amastris became queen over the empire, and Dionysius' two sons, Clearchus and Oxathres – their names, those of their two grandfathers, indicate the cosmopolitan nature of the dynasty – succeeded to the rule of Heracleia, and continued in power until 280, when Lysimachus invaded and executed both.[64] The tyranny coincided with a period of great prosperity: the tyrants were able to steer a course through the difficult politics of the times, retaining the city's independence, and ultimately converted their rule to something indistinguishable from kingship. So Clearchus is not a bad ruler meeting a fateful end, but the first episode in a longer and very successful story.

The reason why all three thinkers struggled so hard to distinguish between 'good' monarchy and 'bad' tyranny was that they inhabited a world in which sole rulers were becoming increasingly important, both as patrons and as forces for social change. Instead of condemning all tyrants out of hand, the philosophers opened a way for accommodation: by learning wisdom, they suggested, a tyrant could potentially transform his rule to that of a virtuous king and be a benefit rather than a burden to his city. This was the approach tried by Plato to Dionysius II (though without conspicuous success), and by Aristotle in his rather warmer relations with the tyrant Hermias of Atarneus. Neither succeeded in creating a philosopher-king, because there was inevitably resistance from the unphilosophically minded mass of the people, and ultimately both were forced to concede their failure. Plato moderated his ideas later in life, while Aristotle returned to considering the interactions of states. Isocrates' purely practical view was no more successful. But the philosophers were right in the long term, if not quite as they intended: monarchy was indeed about to supersede and eclipse popular forms of government.

CHAPTER 5

TYRANTS AND KINGS

I n saying that Sicily was particularly given to one-man rule, Diodorus was introducing Agathocles, the 'last' tyrant of Syracuse (317–289) whom he describes as the bloodiest and most violent of all (Diod. 19.1.8). Agathocles has come down to us as a character of great contradictions: perversely proud of his humble origins as a potter, yet claiming equality with the greatest rulers of his day; so popular that he needed no bodyguard, yet prepared to abandon an entire army to massacre in Africa while he sailed safely home to Sicily. His death, as mentioned in the introduction, was spectacularly gruesome, but most remarkable were the constitutional changes he underwent in the course of his rule: he began as *strategos autocrator* and a tyrant, then proclaimed himself king in 306, striking coins in the name of 'King Agathocles' and marrying a daughter of King Ptolemy I of Egypt. Agathocles has gained his reputation as the 'last tyrant' (and indeed features as the endpoint of many studies) because he is seen as the logical outcome of tyranny: the ruler who is finally able to convert his usurped power into an acknowledged monarchy. After Agathocles, it is suggested, tyrants simply metamorphose into kings and the departure from civic institutions is complete. But while Agathocles may have mingled with the Successor kings and adopted some of their royal symbols, he himself remained aware throughout his long reign of the importance of his relation with the Syracusan *demos*. It is too simple to say that a tyrant could 'become' a king; as Agathocles and other tyrants in this chapter will demonstrate, a tyrant had a personal relationship with the *polis* which he ignored at his peril. Tyranny may have changed in outward appearance in the Hellenistic period, but it remained a purposeful response to a volatile political landscape.

Tyrants and monarchs

Plato and his followers had developed the idea of the good king, the tyrant who uses his power not for self-gratification but to rule for the good of the citizens and bring them to virtue. What they got was entirely different: from the time of Alexander onward monarchy became the dominant form of rule across the Greek world, but the hellenistic kings were self-proclaimed rulers who created huge empires for themselves through conquest and who strove to establish secure dynasties backed by military force. The scale of their power dwarfed the world of the *polis* and they certainly did not rule in anyone's interest but their own: the Ptolemies in Egypt, the Antigonids in Macedonia and Greece and the Seleucids in Asia commanded huge areas and drew enormous revenues from the cities they governed, spending it on conspicuous consumption on a vast scale, hosting glittering courts and founding new cities with spectacular architecture.[65]

The shift to monarchic rule had come about as a consequence of the deeds of Philip and Alexander of Macedon. Philip was the king of Macedonia, a traditional hereditary monarch, and when he began to extend the boundaries of his kingdom in the 340s he tried to weld the areas he conquered into a consolidated kingdom, through the foundation of cities in areas outside Greece, and by diplomacy among the *poleis*. Alexander carried on this policy, albeit over a much wider area: although he had taken over the Persian Empire, and with it some of the style and protocol of the Persian kings, the roots of his legitimacy remained in Macedon. Alexander's death, however, produced a sudden and remarkable change in the political climate in the Greek world. In the thirty years that followed his generals seized whatever parts of his kingdom they could, claiming in an ill-defined and unconstitutional way to be Alexander's heirs. They were not kings 'of' a particular place, or in any line of traditional descent: according to ancient thinking what distinguished a king after Alexander was 'neither descent nor legitimacy ... but the ability to command an army and to handle affairs competently' (Suda s.v. *Basileia*). Some, like Ptolemy in Egypt, found an existing position to occupy – Alexander had been proclaimed Pharaoh in 332 and Ptolemy claimed the title in 305 – but their power was self-created, not established by any constitution. They ruled as kings over whatever territory they could control; indeed Demetrius the Beseiger between 301 and 294 called himself king despite having no kingdom at all (Plut. *Demetr.* 30). Not until 306–5 did the three main successor kings formally adopt the title of *basileus*, but once this was done it raised the possibility for any general with an army to carve out a territory for himself and become a king within Alexander's empire: we find minor kingdoms such as that of the Attalids in Pergamum and of Ophellas in Cyrenaica.

Is this kind of monarchy the logical evolution of tyranny? Some have suggested that tyranny follows a distinct developmental path, from the small-scale tyrant of a single *polis*, via rulers with greater ambitions who created extra-*polis* empires (Dionysius I and Jason of Pherae in particular), culminating in the hellenistic king-by-conquest.[66] According to such theories Dionysius and Clearchus were the prototypes of hellenistic monarchy, and the role of the *polis* in the creation of a tyrant dwindled and vanished through the fourth century. Such a view, however, is viable only from an Aristotelian perspective, assuming that a distinction can be made in constitutional terms between a tyrant and a king, and that it is possible to detect a moment when one becomes the other. But this is to ignore the historical context. Hellenistic monarchy was indeed a new phenomenon, but it is not the case that all tyrants metamorphosed into kings once presented with the opportunity: in fact many were distinctly uneasy about adopting royal titles or symbols. This is because while a Successor king needed no homeland in order to rule, taking his power wherever he (or his army) could find it, a tyrant's power was rooted in a political community. Tyrants were a creation of the *polis* and ruled in concert with the *polis*; they often reshaped a city according to their own will, but even when ruling a wider area, retained their connection with their home city. They needed to be attentive to the people in a way that the Hellenistic kings did not, facing an ever-present possibility of overthrow from within. We will look at three examples to make this relationship clear: first Agathocles, who reveals the complexity of classical Greek ideas about kingship, then the Sicyonian tyrants of the third century, where the pressure of political circumstances actually fostered tyranny, and finally Hieron, famed in our sources as the 'good king' of Sicily, all of whom had to negotiate the distinction between tyranny and monarchy.

Agathocles: traditional or modern?

Agathocles came to power, in good Syracusan tradition, as general in a campaign against Carthage. He generated several myths surrounding his origins – he was supposed to have been exposed as a baby but providentially reunited with his family later on, and his childhood to have been marked by omens of his future greatness – but in fact he rose to prominence again traditionally through military expertise. An oligarchic council of six hundred was in power, and Agathocles positioned himself as a defender of the *demos*; having been elected general he raised an army of supporters, and led a coup in 317. The coup is said to have been extremely violent towards the aristocracy: 4,000 citizens were killed and 6,000 exiled. In the immediate aftermath Agathocles called an assembly and was voted into the position of *strategos autocrator*. A cancellation of debts and redistribution of land followed (Diod. 19.1–9). Despite his initial violence Agathocles proved popular with the *demos* and needed no bodyguard: Polybius (9.23) credits him with 'mild and gentle' rule, and he brought prosperity to Syracuse once more. He was an ambitious and expansionist ruler, attempting to bring the neighbouring Sicilian *poleis* under his sway, and fighting the first Greek campaign against Carthage on their own territory in Africa. While he did succeed in ending the Carthaginian threat to Syracuse, his venture was ultimately damaging: in 306 he faced a mutiny among his soldiers, whereupon, revealing his ruthless streak, he deserted his army, leaving them to their fate in Africa even though they were holding his sons hostage (Justin 8.8–12). The rest of his reign was less ambitious in terms of foreign policy, but he succeeded in bringing Sicily under his rule, and in 304, possibly as a consequence, adopted the title of king. Diodorus says that Agathocles ruled all of Sicily, most of Libya and parts of Italy, though this is an exaggeration; he captured Leucas and Corcyra off the Adriatic coast of Greece and extended his power into Italy with campaigns against Croton and the Bruttii. He was a figure of significance among the Successor kings – his daughter Lanassa was married to Pyrrhus, and he himself married Theoxena, a daughter of Ptolemy I – and his rule lasted for twenty-six years until 289 without significant internal opposition, although we do hear of continued purges of the aristocracy.[67] He seems originally to have intended to pass his power to his son by Theoxene, also named Agathocles, but this sparked a family dispute: his grandson Archagathus (who had hoped to succeed) responded by murdering both Agathocles the grandson and Agathocles the king. On his deathbed Agathocles denounced Archagathus and, rather than see him succeed to the throne, restored power to the *demos*, setting in motion another cycle of civic upheaval (Diod. 21.16).

Should we see Agathocles as the transition point between old-fashioned tyranny and new monarchy, the point where tyrants become kings? He was certainly a traditional tyrant in origin, taking power through class-based *stasis*, and at the beginning of his rule we can identify many features which appear typically tyrannical: the reign of terror in which he disposed of his aristocratic enemies, confiscations of property, cancellation of debts and redistribution of land. Equally, there is no doubt in our sources about the point of change. Diodorus makes a clear statement about Agathocles' assumption of the title of king in 304 and its relation to the actions of Ptolemy, Antigonus and Seleucus:

> When Agathocles learnt that the above-mentioned rulers had adopted the diadem, thinking that he was in no way inferior to them, neither in power nor territory nor achievements, he declared himself a king.
>
> (Diod. 20.54.1)

The shift to monarchy is also seen to be reflected in Agathocles' coinage. At the start of his reign, between 317 and 310, the coins minted had carried traditional Syracusan imagery with the legend SYRAKOSIÔN (of the Syracusans), distinguished from previous issues only by the addition of a small three-legged symbol (triskeles). After 310, however, Agathocles began to develop his own distinctive coin types, producing silver and gold coins, some imitating Ptolemy's designs, with the legend AGATHOKLEIOUS (of Agathocles). The bronze coinage retained the name of the Syracusans in this period. Later coins, after 304, see the legend AGATHOKLES BASILEUS appearing on the gold and bronze coinage with the head of Athena or Artemis and the winged thunderbolt.[68] Presented in this way the coins tell a story of gradually increasing control as Agathocles took over minting privileges from the Syracusans and used the title of king, modelling his coins on his Successor peers and finally pushing out any civic form of coinage, making concrete the growth of royal power.

But what exactly a shift from tyranny to monarchy might entail is hard to pin down. According to some, the relationship between the king and the assembly was formalised and his heir presented for their approval; but this demonstrates that the assembly continued to function unchanged, and indeed a papyrus fragment records a debate in the assembly at the time of the Libyan campaign.[69] Similarly the interpretation of the coins is not straightforward: Syracuse had a long tradition of civic coinage which Agathocles could not simply change for his own types. Syracusan types continue even alongside the coins proclaiming AGATHOKLES BASILEUS. After Agathocles' resignation and death the restored democracy used his types with the legend SYRAKOSIÔN, as well as creating new types of their own depicting Zeus Eleutherios.[70] Moreover Agathocles showed considerable restraint when it came to presenting himself as a king. The Successors had adopted the a diadem (a simple woollen headband) as a symbol of their royal power, and Agathocles could have followed this practice, but according to Diodorus (20.54) he rejected the diadem in favour of a wreath, worn by virtue of a priesthood of Olympian Zeus. He prided himself on not using a bodyguard and cultivated an unassuming attitude in public, hardly the acts of a Ptolemy or a Seleucus. There is, nevertheless, also an indication that he had adopted other forms of royal privilege even before his claim to kingship: an odd occasion in 309 during a mutiny on his African campaign has Agathocles wearing a cloak of royal purple as he confronted the soldiers (Diod. 20.34.4). Why such a confusing use of monarchic symbolism?

The answer can be found by looking to the other precedents for Agathocles' rule: the Greek tyrants of the fourth century who had struggled with precisely this issue of self-presentation. Dionysius of Syracuse was called a tyrant by his contemporaries, yet he himself used the title '*Archon* of Sicily' to describe his position, and adopted some royal forms: the tent of purple and gold at Olympia, the chariot drawn by white horses in which he drove to his wedding, and the mysteriously named 'royal gate' where he was buried. Later writers use the term *basileus* to describe Dionysius, and Oost has argued that all the Syracusan tyrants were known in their own time as kings.[71] Other rulers found different methods of expressing their power in practical terms, such as Clearchus, tyrant of Heracleia. Justin (16.5.8–10) tells us that in the 350s his rule took on a distinctly monarchic character, shown by his outward actions. He declared himself to be the son of Zeus, and when appearing in public dressed in purple robes, a gold crown and the boots of a stage king; he also had a gilded eagle carried in front of him as a sign of his divine descent.[72] The nature of Clearchus' rule had not changed, only his means of expressing it, but what is striking is that he was 'dressing up' as a king, assuming a costume based on the clothes appropriate to a monarch from the theatre. This implies that there were few formal signifiers of monarchy in the Greek tradition, so a ruler like Clearchus had to invent his own, taking them from dramatic or historical representations. He could not step into a recognised set of features which made a king, but wove elements around himself from what was available, as did all fourth-century rulers. Dionysius I had similarly adopted symbolism from Persia and from mythology: with no precedent of royal rule tyrants had to create a representation of their own. Agathocles was also operating within this tradition, and this is why he appears to be dressing as a king before his formal assumption of the title – he did not embark on a completely new set of behaviours in 306, but took a public step to align himself with the Successors. The public proclamation of the kingship was the novelty, as hinted in the sources' emphasis on the use of the title in letters and inscriptions. That he rejected other elements of their monarchic show indicates that he was most concerned to present himself as ruler within Syracuse, not on an undifferentiated world stage.

Hellenistic monarchy had developed its particular form to meet the challenges faced by the Successors of Alexander: establishing their legitimacy in lands where they had none, ruling large and diverse empires, and creating institutions to implement and assert their power. This was not what Agathocles was trying to do, because Sicily had not formed part of Alexander's empire. Alexander's campaign had taken him east, from Macedonia to India; although his 'last plans' recorded in Diodorus suggested that he might subsequently have looked west, Magna Graecia was distant from his influence. Hence it was not possible for any western Greek ruler to be, in a strict sense, a 'successor'. Agathocles was thus not trying to give his reign legitimacy in the style of the Successors because he was neither a conqueror and nor an outsider. Greek tyrants, unlike the Successors, came to power within existing political structures and were forced to negotiate with them: while it is common to suggest that the tyrant stood in opposition to the institutions of the city, as we have seen most tyrants in fact co-existed with such institutions. We hear of tyrants who altered the constitution of their state to democracy or oligarchy, or who created new citizens, but not of any who swept away all other forms of government: there are references in the reigns of Pisistratus, the Dionysii and Agathocles to assemblies and magistrates. Indeed the family of the tyrant often proved valuable for this very reason. The idea that Agathocles could step outside Syracuse and rearrange his power as monarch ignores the fact that the city was the locus of his power: for all his control over Sicily and his wider empire he remained parochial in his concerns (as had his predecessors), building in Syracuse (Diod. 16.83.2) and courting the *demos* there.

To interpret Agathocles' position as both tyrant and king offers a fresh perspective. We no longer need to look for a 'breakthrough moment' allowing Agathocles to think of himself as a king and to require others to do so: he may always have done that. What we see is rather the imitative expression of power; if kingship in fourth-century Greece seems to be about outward show rather then constitutional change, this is because it was – a tyranny was never a fixed constitutional role, but always a process of negotiation with civic institutions, and self-presentation was an important part of this. It is plain that Agathocles did not bring about a fundamental change in the political landscape since after his abdication and death a democracy took control for a short time, until Hicetas was elected to the *strategia* to end the fighting after Agathocles' assassination and ruled for nine years to 279. Later Thoenon and Sosistratus overthrew Hicetas and divided power in Syracuse between themselves. Between 278 and 276 Pyrrhus came to Sicily and ruled as king, though many sources say that he became a despot, and after his withdrawal was to come the last and most successful of classical Syracusan rulers, Hieron II.[73] Agathocles' declaring himself a king had not turned Syracuse into a monarchy: the *polis* continued to struggle to find the most effective form of government.

Mainland Greece: tyrants and tyrannicides

On the mainland the Successor kings brought about a new 'age of tyranny': Polybius (2.41) claims that no one created more tyrants than Antigonus II Gonatas (283–240), particularly in the Peloponnese. This can be seen at Sicyon, which furnished our exemplary constitutional history in the introduction: in the third century Pausanias lists no fewer than six Sicyonian tyrants, the last of whom, Nicocles, was overthrown by their greatest leader, Aratus

(Paus. 2.8.1–3). Aratus himself has an intriguing reputation as a tyrant-slayer despite taking power in a violent coup and holding the *strategia* seventeen times in the course of thirty-three years. The reasons for such a proliferation of tyrants are to be found in the political circumstances of Greece after Alexander. From 338 and the conquest of Greece by Philip the *poleis* had been continuously under the domination of an external power, which had an effect on their internal politics. When Philip began to expand his power he attempted to ally himself with individual *poleis*, supporting political parties favourable to Macedon, and this is what underlies the accusations of Demosthenes that Philip established tyrannies across Greece. The Successor kings, because they were in competion with one another and were keen to gain the loyalty of the states in Greece, followed the same pattern. They held no particular political convictions, and would support democrats or oligarchs if they thought it beneficial to their cause, but just as Philip and Alexander had, they found tyranny the most attractive form of government. This is because of the personal nature of Hellenistic monarchy: the men who became kings at the head of an army rarely had an existing system of government to fit into, and were thus forced to create their own, such that it could deal with the diverse nations and cities which they ruled. This was done largely through the institution of 'Friends', individuals chosen by a king for their abilities who acted as officials, generals, ambassadors or counsellors, in the absence of a more formal governing group.[74] The relation between a Greek city and a king was most often mediated through personal connection: a city would send a representative who had a personal link with the king, and the king would dispense benefactions (in the form of money, grain or marks of favour) through that individual. Kings therefore found dealing with tyrants much easier than with oligarchic or democratic governments, and (as Demosthenes shows) politicians within such systems who developed personal relationships with a king found it hard to refute accusations of bribery or corruption. Tyranny thus suited both sides very well, giving the king a known figure with whom to deal and the tyrant a source of power to tap. A tyrant who owed his position to a king would obviously be even more useful politically.

We should not make the mistake, however, of casting the Greek cities as politically passive, at best allowing whichever existing party could gain Macedonian favour taking power unopposed, and at worst suffering the imposition of a Macedonian-chosen ruler, with the citizens playing no role in the government of their own state. This is not what appears to have happened at Sicyon. The accounts of events are confusing since they are drawn ultimately from the memoirs of Aratus himself, and hence are very one-sided, but the political background is nevertheless clear. By 303 Sicyon had fallen under the domination of Antigonus I. The Macedonian overlords demolished the original city and rebuilt it as a new *polis* on the acropolis, to strengthen a key defensive point (Diod. 20.102); the city was, according to Plutarch, no longer ruled as an aristocracy, but fell under a succession of tyrants. First came Cleon, then Timocleidas and Euthydemus together, who were deposed by Cleinias, father of Aratus. Cleinias was killed by Abantidas who then became tyrant, and he was succeeded in turn by his father Paseas. Paseas was murdered by Nicocles, who was overthrown by Aratus (Plut. *Arat.* 2–3). Such a dizzying succession of rulers implies a period of great unrest and instability, and the struggles between tyrants are cast in ideological terms: Cleinias is described as a 'champion of the *demos*', and according to Plutarch was actually elected, along with Timocleidas, as chief magistrate of a new government (*Arat.* 2.1.). This may be tendentious (as the father of Aratus, Cleinias' reputation needed to be suitably democratic), but it implies a role for the people which went beyond passive acceptance of a Macedonian-favoured ruler. Furthermore the relationships between tyrants and tyrannicides were surprisingly close: Plutarch reveals in his account of Cleinias' death at the hands of Abantidas that notwithstanding their hostility, Cleinias' brother was married to Abantidas' sister, suggesting that we may be looking at a traditional type of power struggle within the Sicyonian aristocracy. In a situation where wealthy men were battling to take control of the city the kings were a resource to be exploited, and certainly Aratus can be seen to have inherited friendships with both Antigonus and Ptolemy, suggesting that his family cultivated the attachments.

Aratus is remembered in our sources as the greatest Sicyonian leader ever, yet the nature of his power is contradictory. After his father's death the seven-year-old Aratus had been spirited away to safety in Argos, and on reaching adulthood he gathered a group of exiles and returned to Sicyon to overthrow the ruling tyrant, Nicocles. This is presented very much as an ideologically motivated liberation of the city, but clearly Aratus was attempting to restore his family's place at the heart of civic politics. Plutarch gives a very detailed account of the coup, drawn from Aratus' own memoirs (including the difficulty encountered by the conspirators in slipping past the gardener's dog), and does his best to characterise the coup as a liberation: on entering Sicyon Aratus proclaimed that he 'summoned the citizens to freedom', while in the course of the attack not one man was killed or wounded, not even Nicocles who managed to escape through a secret tunnel (Plut. *Arat.* 5–9). But although the city was liberated, Aratus continued to act very much as an individual ruler: his first act was to restore the exiles who had fled the previous tyranny, something which caused great unrest as the exiles attempted to reclaim the property they had lost. He was then appointed as arbiter of the disputes with absolute powers, and his response was not a civil but a personal one: he sailed to Egypt and used his connections with Ptolemy II Philadelphos to get 150 talents of money as a 'gift', which he distributed in Sicyon to resolve the property disputes, indicating a personal power (*Arat.* 13–14).

Aratus is also credited with sole responsibility for bringing Sicyon into the Achaean League in 251, thus laying the foundation of the city's third-century power. The League had existed since the archaic period as a local organisation of Achaean cities, but Aratus realised its potential and induced the Sicyonians to join. He was soon appointed general and began to direct League strategy, holding office as *strategos* every other year (the maximum permitted) for most of the rest of his life. He expanded the League partly by persuasion and partly by force, leading a daring campaign to recapture the Acrocorinth from Macedon, and persuaded the tyrants of Megara, Hermione and Phlius to abdicate and join the League (Plut. *Arat.* 18–23, Polyb. 2.43–4). His actions are presented as a personal crusade against tyranny, upholding the values of Greek democracy and liberty against Macedonian control by tyrants. Indeed Plutarch recounts that Aratus hated tyranny so much that when he 'freed the city' he destroyed all the previous tyrants' portraits, except for a portrait of the fourth-century ruler Aristratus by Melanthus and Apelles. He was impressed by the artistry of the picture, but ultimately his hatred of tyranny won through, and he ordered that it be destroyed. In a bid to save such a work of art his friend the painter Nealces offered to remove just the figure of Aristratus from the painting, allowing the rest to be preserved. So Nealces replaced Aristratus with a palm tree, although he accidentally left Aristratus' feet still in the picture underneath a chariot. (*Arat.* 13). Yet there is more to Aratus' actions than a simple determination to wipe out tyranny: when Lydiades of Megalopolis stood down from power in 235 he very rapidly appears as a general of the League, and someone with whom Aratus had a significant rivalry: we still seem to be in a scenario of elite competition. Similarly Aratus' attempts to liberate Argos from its tyrants met considerable opposition from the citizens who clearly did not share his view of the regime (*Arat.* 25–7, 29, 35). One can cast the story, as do Plutarch and Polybius, as Aratus' desire to end tyranny, or one can read it as a tale of competing aristocrats, repeating the struggles of the previous generation of Sicyonian politics.

The later part of Aratus' career bears out the view of his commitment to power rather than policy: finding the League seriously threatened by the Spartans under their king Cleomenes, Aratus suddenly reversed his anti-Macedonian stance and brokered a deal with Antigonus II for alliance in return for the restoration of the Acrocorinth. This was essentially a private venture ratified by the League, and Aratus subsequently became an intimate friend of the Macedonian king and an advisor to his son Demetrius (*Arat.* 43–6). These events reveal the extent to which the Greek cities were dependent on the kings for security and prosperity, but also the way in which the pressures of the new situation favoured individual rule. In a world of vast new kingdoms the *polis* was too small to compete on its own terms, and only a supranational organisation could muster the manpower and wealth necessary to carve out a measure of independence. Such an organisation (of which there were several) demands a single leader, at least in warfare, and we are not far away from the model of the League of Corinth with Philip at its head. It is not that Aratus actually was sole leader, though his actions indicate the ambition, but that disputes within the League hierarchy were divisive and damaging, whereas strong direction by one leader was the route to success. If we contrast Aratus with his predecessors Pericles (in Athens) and Epaminondas (in Boeotia) it is easy to see how the institutions of the *polis* worked to limit individual ambitions: both Pericles and Epaminondas held the position of *strategos* or *Boiotarch* as often as they were able, but both were subject to the rule of the state, Pericles working alongside rivals and an assembly which could easily depose him, and Epaminondas with six colleagues, and likewise an assembly that could (and did) put him on trial.[75] Aratus was a Sicyonian, with Sicyonian interests at heart, but operating in a wider and looser framework because personal relationships with the kings were vitally important for the League, but also brought the potential for individual action.

Hieron and Rome: the true 'end of tyranny'

Neither Agathocles nor Aratus was the last Greek tyrant: that honour actually belongs to Hieron II, the last great ruler of Syracuse, who in a way brings this study full circle since he chose to associate his rule very strongly with the tyrants of the past. Hieron is presented in our sources unequivocally as a king, yet even he, we are told, was reluctant to adopt the dress and manner of a monarch. He ruled for fifty-four years, living to an impressive age of ninety-one, and our sources lavish praise on his character (and that of his son Gelon), suggesting that he combined modesty and self-control with traditional values and wisdom. Hieron is the point at which tyranny and kingship become difficult to distinguish, but not for the reasons that we might think.

Only Polybius preserves an account of Hieron's rise to power, but the events are familiar: he began as a commander of the Syracusan army which was in a state of mutiny, was smuggled into the city by his supporters and gained the ascendancy over his opponents. 'He then administered affairs so mildly and generously that the Syracusans ... unanimously approved Hieron's appointment as *strategos*.' (Polyb.1.8.4) Even at this point his ambition extended beyond the *strategia* and he married Philistis, daughter of the aristocratic Leptines. He then led a successful campaign against the Mamertines, a group of Campanian mercenaries who had established themselves at Messana from where they launched raids on the surrounding area, and on his return to Syracuse he was hailed as king. Polybius says that the coup was achieved without killing or injuring a single citizen, and that although he later tried on several occasions to lay down power, he was prevented from doing so by the assembly (Polyb. 1.8.9). Just as with Aratus, our accounts of Hieron are universally favourable: he is presented as a man of noble and unassuming character and a mild and gentle ruler who governed in the best interests of the citizens, despite his fairly naked climb to power. The biggest factor in the peace and prosperity which he brought to Syracuse was undoubtedly the treaty which he signed with Rome in 263; Rome guaranteed his authority and in exchange he offered his unstinting support against Carthage, providing huge amounts of corn and other supplies. In 216, for instance, he sent to the Romans a golden statue of Victory along with 300,000 measures of wheat and 200,000 of barley; these gifts of grain were what made him such a valued ally. As with the cities of the Greek mainland subordination to a greater power meant that foreign policy was closed to Hieron, and he was able to devote his attention to the domestic economy; Polybius refers to a life led among affluence and lavish expenditure, and Hieron was also able to attract to his court such figures as Archimedes, whom he employed to create novel weapons including the famous 'burning mirrors' used to set fire to enemy ships.[76]

Like Agathocles, Hieron's use of royal insignia was mixed. He minted coins which carried not only his name but a portrait as well, and also produced coins in the name of his wife Philistis with the title of queen (*basilissa*), though the coinage of the Syracusan state carried on alongside.[77] But both Hieron and Gelon are distinctly said to have been 'distinguished by no outward mark of royalty', that is, no purple clothing, no diadem and no bodyguard. Hieron in fact sought legitimacy for his rule through connections with past Syracusan tyrants: naming his son and daughter Gelon and Damarete was the most obvious of his actions, and he created a whole series of links with the Deinomenid tyrants as well as with the Dionysii. The

Deinomenids especially were remembered very positively (Plutarch *Mor.* 551f–552a reveals a tradition remembering them as noble, wise and beneficent rulers), and Hieron's father Heroclitus was claimed to have been a descendent of that family. There is an interesting recasting of history by the first-century Diodorus who tells the story of the Syracusan *demos*' acclamation of Gelon I in 479 after his victory at Himera. Gelon, we are told, summoned the people to an assembly fully armed, and

> appeared before them not only unarmed, but without even a tunic, wearing only a cloak, and stepping forward he gave an account of his life and deeds on behalf of the Syracusans. The crowd shouted their approval at each deed that he mentioned, and were amazed that he had entrusted himself unarmed to anyone who might wish to kill him, so much so that they not ony did not punish him for having taken the tyranny, but with one voice hailed him as their benefactor, saviour and king.
>
> (Diod. 11.26.5–6)

Given the very Hellenistic terms used to describe Gelon, it may be that Hieron's story has been retrojected onto Gelon (a 'good' ruler) to prefigure Hieron's own actions, positioning him within a tradition of successful rulership. The later historian Justin records a lengthy list of omens which were supposed to have foretold his future greatness, all of which appear to be modelled on previous rulers. For instance, the infant Hieron was supposed to have been exposed at birth but saved by a swarm of bees who brought honey to feed him, leading his father to reclaim him on the advice of the soothsayers, a story which refers to tales of both Agathocles and Dionysius I. Another omen is given in a strangely abbreviated form; one day when Hieron was at school a wolf appeared and seized his writing-tablet. This is an incomplete echo of the story told of Gelon, who chased the wolf which had seized his tablet, and thus escaped death in a sudden earthquake which destroyed the building (above p. 54).[78] The reuse of omens in this way demonstrates that Hieron and his citizens saw the history of Syracuse as a source of legitimacy, not as a series of wicked usurping tyrants within a cradling democracy.

That Hieron wanted to reach back into the past implies that he was not trying to be a king in the Hellenistic sense, but rather a legitimate civic ruler. The implication of the story of his unsuccessful attempts to abdicate is that he ruled by the consent of the popular assembly, and certainly when he died his successor Hieronymus needed the approval of the assembly before he took control. But the events of Hieronymus' brief reign show the real reason for Hieron's presentation as a king. Hieron was remembered so favourably largely because of his pro-Roman policies; there is a fundamental shift in our sources at this time, from Greek to Roman, and Hieron becomes a part of the history of Rome. Roman historians had, inevitably, a different outlook on the politics of the Greeks: the battle of ideologies and names between democrats, oligarchs, tyrants and generals was closed to them, and they tended to accept foreign kings at their own valuation. The anomalies of Hieron's position, as a usurping commander and yet a king, were of little interest to Roman writers; his loyalty in the war with Carthage was what counted. Thus Hieron and his children shade imperceptibly into kings, not because their constitutional position changed or the nature of their rule, but because history changed around them. Hieronymus, who rejected Rome in favour of new alliance with Carthage, gained a reputation in history which is entirely negative, dwelling on his cruelty, luxury and weakness. He survived for only nine months before he was assassinated by a pro-Roman conspiracy and Syracuse threatened to dissolve once more into *stasis*, but this time it was conquered for Rome by Marcellus, ending independent Syracusan history in classical times.

Sicily became a Roman province in 212, ending 500 years of Syracusan history, while the rest of the Greek states moved gradually from the power of the Hellenistic kings into the the expanding empire of Rome, culminating in the Sack of Corinth in 146. Greek history became Roman history and the tyrants vanished. This, though, is a function of historiography rather than history: Roman writers were concerned with the terms of their own political debate (in which kingship was contrasted to republicanism) and less so with what they encountered abroad: kings, tyrants and *archons* were all one to them. They encountered Greek ideas about politics, but only as abstract and specialised; not until the late Republic would thinkers such as Cicero, under the extreme circumstances of the Triumvirates, start to use Plato's ideas as a means to describe and understand what was happening around them.[79] But even though the *polis* had proven ineffective as a political form in an era of nation-states and kingdoms, tyranny had turned out to be an effective choice of government to meet the challenges of the age. Leadership in warfare, personal connections with the kings, ambition and vision: tyrants could offer all of these, and under leaders such as Agathocles, Aratus and Hieron, cities were able to go on prospering in a difficult world.

CONCLUSION

W e have considered tyranny throughout this book from the point of view of the tyrant, and of political philosophers, but what about the opinion of the *demos*? Did the people of an ancient city simply wake up one day to find a tyrant occupying the Acropolis and their freedom gone? Did they vote in a tyrant, either because they were naïve or because they were under military pressure to do so, and then spend the rest of their lives chafing under the despotic yoke? Did they resent the idea of life led under tyranny and yearn to be free? Considering tyranny from the citizen's point of view provides an interesting antidote to some of the assumptions which underlie ideas about ancient political life.

To begin with, was it possible for an individual to become tyrant without popular consent? That the *demos* played an essential part in the creation of a tyrant is very clear in our sources: Sicilian tyrants are elected *strategos autocrator*, or later, hailed as kings, at assemblies; rulers are appointed as *diallaktes* (as with Clearchus) or *aisymnetes* (as Pittacus); an heir who takes power is presented to the assembly for their approval (as with Dionysius II). The consent of the *demos* was necessary for a tyrant to take power, but why should the *demos* take this step if it was plainly to their detriment? In Diodorus' account of Agathocles' appointment he gives clear reasons: many of the citizens at the assembly were implicated in Agathocles' original coup and were hoping to escape justice by making him ruler; others were poor and indebted and hoped to gain from economic reform. The 'uncorrupted' citizens were a minority, and were simply too cowed by the mob to show their dissent. Lavelle paints a similar picture of the assembly in Athens in 560:

> Happily deceived by Peisistratos' promises, plied by Megakles' agents, favorably inclined toward Pisistratos for his war record anyway, and perhaps taken in by the power of his oratory on the occasion ... the demos voted Peisistratos what he (and Megakles) needed to establish his tyranny.

Arguments like this, however, do ancient voters a disservice. Were there no reasons why the *demos* might have wanted a tyrant?[80]

The institutions of *aisymneteia*, *diallakteia* and dictatorship show that the appointment of an individual to lead a city in the face of a particular challenge was a universal remedy across the ancient world: in times of threat from an enemy or of disruption from within, all states saw the virtue in giving power to one person who could direct affairs or create new laws with a single vision. It has been noted before how the figure of the lawgiver, such as a Solon or a Demonax, appointed to redraft the constitution, shades very easily into that of the tyrant: in order to redraft the constitution a lawgiver had to be given extraordinary powers, and many tyrants reformed the laws or constitution as part of their rule. The Roman dictator, appointed with complete control over army and state, falls into the same category, and Dionysius of Halicarnassus refers to the dictatorship explicitly as an 'elected tyranny'. Such figures appear throughout the history of the *polis*, and even seem to form spontaneously by the will of the people. There is a strong tendency in all states for leaders who become successful and popular to be re-elected into office as or more frequently than permitted, enabling them to direct policy: Pericles, Epaminondas and Aratus are all leaders of this type, which has its counterpart in Rome in 18 BC, when a reluctant Augustus was pressured by the people to take up the dictatorship.[81]

Linked to the desire for clear leadership is the economic benefit
of tyranny. The archaic tyrants all presided over increasing revenues
and the monumentalisation of their states, though it has often
been claimed that they were successful only indirectly, because they
ruled at a time of increasing prosperity generally. But the longer
perspective offered by this book shows that tyrannically-ruled states
of all periods tended to be both successful and expansionist: single-
handed control could have benefits in terms of organisation (taxation,
the creation of large-scale economic resources such as harbours or
roads, and engagement with the outside world). Despite Aristotle's
claim that tyrants' building projects were a means to subjugate and
impoverish the citizens, it is under tyranny that we find many of the
great temples, public buildings and monuments being constructed.
A tyrant was often Isocrates' 'man of vision and spirit' who had a
plan for the development of his state coupled with the power to put
it into practice – one might think of the prosperity of Samos under
Polycrates, or of Thessaly under Jason – and tyranny also offered
the stability to enable long-term planning. Many sources dwell on
tyrants' schemes for extracting money from their long-suffering
citizens, but an alternative interpretation of this is to recognise that
a tyrant had the ability to impose financial demands: contributions
for the public good, whether building fortifications or developing
a harbour; contrast the despair of a Demosthenes at his fellow-
citizens' unwillingness to divert their Theoric Fund to support the
war against Macedonia. In both these contexts a sole ruler could
avoid the situation of competing political leaders (described so
effectively by Thucydides) in which self-interest and the pursuit of
popularity distorted policy.

It is also worth reflecting on the ways in which tyrants were
expelled from power. As emphasised above, many tyrants died in
their beds and were succeeded by members of their family, but
all dynasties came to an end at some stage. The Athenian-based

model – the *demos* attain political maturity and overthrow the tyrants – is very powerful (especially for an idea which is untrue), but in fact the tyrant removed by a popular uprising is very rare. Tyrants were frequently removed by external powers (such as the Thessalian rulers by Macedonia, or Euphron by the Arcadians) or by rival rulers (as in the case of Dionysius II and Dion) but rarely by a pure popular uprising.[82] The fundamental reason for this is a lack of political consciousness among the *demos*: with no conception of themselves as an enfranchised group, they had no system to establish in a tyranny's place. Expelling a tyrant would merely create a vacuum to be filled by another aristocratic leader. This was particularly the case because tyrants did not suppress existing civic institutions: under most, magistrates continued to be elected and assemblies held. It is easy to say that an assembly held under these circumstances was a mere formality, in that no one would dare to contradict the tyrant's will, but the tyrant needed the agreement of the people and could not simply dictate policy. When Dionysius I wanted to go to war, for instance, he had to win over the assembly before he could do so because it was the citizens who would both pay for the war and, more importantly, fight the battles: Dionysius could not simply require them to follow his lead.[83] The relationship between tyrant and *demos* was always the central point of concern for rulers because it allowed both sides to sidestep the influence of the aristocracy.

It would be naïve, however, to ignore the negative side of tyranny, the cruelties and atrocities on which our ancient sources dwell – purges of enemies, killing of aristocrats, seizing of property and exiling. While ancient tyrants were not the monsters which historians have made them, neither were they always 'mild and gentle' to their opponents. It was, however, chiefly the upper classes who bore the brunt of tyrannical oppression, since these were the individuals felt to pose a threat to the tyrant's position (and the evidence of conspiracies tends to prove this right). Killing and exiling of potential opponents was frequent under tyranny, but classical Greece was a violent society, and political rivalry frequently took this form under other constitutions too. Stories of attacks by tyrants on the *demos* are much fewer, and tend to be vague and extreme, such as the claim by Theopompus (*FGrH* 115 F181) that under Clearchus the citizens of Heracleia regularly took an antidote to guard against poisoning by aconite. We should not confuse ancient tyrants with their modern counterparts: we do not find tyrants committing genocide on an industrial scale, or dictators who systematically impoverish their country for personal gain. The *polis* was a comparatively tiny political community, and acts of true horror or sacrilege attracted condemnation and action from all around.

We have seen how in many cases a tyrant led his or her state to expansion and empire, or to prosperity; we have encountered tyrants who were orderers and lawgivers. Yet the expectation is still that all this can have meant nothing to the *demos* compared to their political freedom. Any city under a tyrant is supposed to have been impatient for liberty, and every tyrant to have faced a daily struggle for survival. Such a view derives in part from the assertions of ancient philosophers that tyranny was an undesirable state, but more especially from a set of assumptions about Greek political life which are fundamentally based on Athens in 432. Pericles (as represented by Thucydides) boldly asserts in the *Funeral Oration* that politics is the business of every citizen, and the implicit assumption is that the existence of a tyrant deprived every individual of his political rights, but in most *poleis* this was never true. Almost all Greek *poleis*, even those calling themselves democracies, operated a property qualification for citizenship, if not a birth qualification too, and most inhabitants of *poleis* were disenfranchised as a matter of course because they were too poor. Only at Athens and one or two other places was politics even theoretically open to all. In this context it is easier to understand the appeal of a tyrant who promised to bypass existing constitutional limitations and include the whole of the city in his domain; the decision of the *demos* need not be a foolish or mistaken one, but one made in their own best interests.

A longer view of tyranny, such as we have taken here, offers a fresh historical perspective. Current practice encourages a view of ancient history in which Pisistratus looms very large while Agathocles is forgotten, and in which Jason of Pherae is barely known, while the Cypselids are familiar. This arises partly from concentration on a small number of sources, and partly from the adoption of a linear view of historical development: what emerges is a simple narrative of archaic tyranny – democracy – Athenian Empire – Philip of Macedon – Hellenistic kingship. Two features make this a particular distortion in the case of tyranny: the neglect of events in the fourth century, and the general exclusion of Sicily and the West from consideration. But more seriously, some profound underlying convictions about ancient politics need to be exposed and challenged. This book has emphasised the fluidity of constitutions in the Greek *polis* – the idea that change was normal and stability elusive. Yet much thinking about tyranny rests on the unspoken assumption that there was a 'normal' constitution in every *polis*, a democratic or broadly oligarchic constitution which was its natural state, and that while political change might take place, the state would sooner or later revert to its basic form. This again derives from fifth-century Athenian experience; in this case two short-lived oligarchies interrupted the continuing democracy, which proved robust enough to last until 322. But the constitutions of most *poleis* were much less stable: how to maintain a constitution is, after all, Aristotle's primary concern in the *Politics*. The experiences of Sicyon

and Syracuse indicate that a state would undergo a succession of
constitutional types, in which each leader or leaders would start
afresh, redefining the constitution and their own position within
it. There is no 'reversion' to a natural form at the end of a period
of tyranny, nor a natural form to which to revert: at each moment
those who held power were making their own rules.

From this perspective the place of tyranny within Greek
politics takes on a different complexion. There is neither a linear
development – an 'age of tyrannies' followed by political maturity
– nor the situation in which settled constitutions were disrupted
by episodes of tyranny. Tyranny was not a phase through which a
polis passed, but a permanent option, for the citizens as much as
for the would-be ruler, because it offered answers to some of the
difficult questions of government: how to make the state unified
in purpose and efficient, how to bring stability and how to control
the disruptive competition for power among the wealthy. The Greek
tyrants may have come down to us through moralising historians
as self-interested and cruel, their lurid stories serving as a terrible
warning, but their achievements show that there was no one like a
tyrant for getting things done.

NOTES

1. History of Sicyon: Paus. 2.5.6, Hdt. 6.126–30, Thuc. 5.81, Xen. *Hell.* 7.1.44–6, 7.3, Dem. 17.16, 18.48, 294–5, Diod. 20.102, Paus. 2.8.1–3. In general on Sicyon, see A. Griffin, *Sikyon* (Oxford 1982).
2. The Cypselids are discussed in chapter 1, Dionysius and Mausolus in chapter 3 and Demetrius of Phaleron in chapter 4.
3. The term 'dictator', like 'tyrant', was originally the name of a magistrate elected in a time of crisis – for a period of up to six months – with complete power over the state. It had no negative connotations for the Romans until the time of Julius Caesar, whose attempt to hold a permanent dictatorship in Rome led to his assassination.
4. See chapter 4, pp. 92–5.
5. On the development of ideas about tyranny, see V. Parker, '*Tyrannos*: the semantics of a political concept from Archilochus to Aristotle', *Hermes* 126 (1998) 145–172 and J.L. O'Neill, 'The semantic usage of *tyrannos* and related words', *Antichthon* 20 (1986) 26–40. Historical treatment of Agathocles: Polybius 12.15 and Diodorus 21.17; Philistus: B. Caven, *Dionysius I: warlord of Sicily* (New Haven and London 1990) 1; Athenian laws against tyranny: M. Ostwald, 'The Athenian legislation against tyranny and subversion', *TAPA* 86 (1955) 103–28.
6. Discussed in chapter 4 below.
7. Aristotle *Politics* 1310a 39 – b 14, 1310b 40–1311a 22.
8. Pisistratus: Hdt. 1.61–4; Dionysius I: Diod. 13.91–6; Pittacus of Miletus: Arist. *Politics* 1285a 29ff.; Pheidon of Argos: Arist. *Politics* 1310b 26–8; Demetrius of Phaleron: Diod. 18.74.3; Mausolus and Artemisia: Diod. 15.90.2–3, 16.36.2.
9. Reconstruction of the dynasty is contoversial: see Griffin, *Sikyon* 40–3 and N. Hammond, 'The family of Orthagoras', *CQ* 6 (1956), 45–53.
10. 'Thirty Tyrants': Arist. *Rhet.* 1401a34, Lysias 12.35; see P. Krentz, *The Thirty at Athens* (Ithaca 1982).

11. Historical kings: R. Drews, *Basileus: evidence for kingship in Geometric Greece* (New Haven and London 1983), T. Kelly, *A History of Argos* (Minneapolis 1976) ch. 7.

12. See J.M. Hall, *A History of the Archaic Greek World* (Oxford 2007) ch. 6, with further reading.

13. On the (empty) beehive as a suitable hiding place see D. Ogden, *The Crooked Kings of Ancient Greece* (London 1997) 88–9.

14. Herodotus 5.91–2a–f, Nicolaus of Damascus *FGrH* 90 fr. 58. See J.B.Salmon, *Wealthy Corinth* (Oxford 1984), ch. 15.

15. Melanchros: Diog. Laert. *Lives of the Philosophers* 1.74; Pittacus: Alcaeus frs.117, 128, 129, 306, 332, 348; Arist. *Pol.* 1285a29–40.; Nicolaus of Damascus *FGrH* 90 fr. 53. See R. Osborne, *Greece in the Making* (London 2002) pp 190–7.

16. Miletus: Arist. *Pol.* 1305a 15–18; Pheidon: *Pol.* 1310b 26–7; Pittacus: *Pol.* 1285a 29–40, Dion. Hal. 5.73, Strabo *Geog.* 13.2.3; Pittacus as lawgiver: Arist. *Pol.* 1274b 18–23.

17. See P. Millett, 'Hesiod and his world', *PCPS* 210 (1984) 84–115.

18. See K.A. Raaflaub, 'Soldiers, citizens and the evolution of the early Greek *polis*', in L.G. Mitchell and P.J. Rhodes (eds), *The Development of the Polis in Archaic Greece* (London 1997) 49–59, with further references, and G.L. Cawkwell, 'Early Greek tyranny and the people', *CQ* 45 (1995) 73–86. Orthagoras as *mageiros*: Diod. 8.24 (= Fornara 10).

19. See Salmon, *Wealthy Corinth* 136–7 and 202; Arist. fr. 611.20; G. Shipley, *A History of Samos* (Oxford 1984) p.76.

20. Leadership in war: Pheidon, Hdt. 6.127.3; Cleisthenes, Hdt. 5.67–8 and A. Griffin, *Sikyon* (Oxford 1982) 50–54; Cypselus, Nicolaus of Damascus *FGrH* 90 fr. 57; Pisistratus, Hdt. 1.59.4. Cypselid colonies: Nicolaus of Damascus *FGrH* 90 frs. 57–9. Building projects: Cypselids, Ar. *Pol.* 1313b 22–3, Salmon, *Wealthy Corinth* 133–4, 227–9; Polycrates: Shipley, *History of Samos* ch.5; Pisistratids: [Plato] *Hipparchos* 228c (roads); Thuc. 2.16, Pausanias 1.14.1 (fountain-house); Cleisthenes: Griffin, *Sikyon* 106–111.

21. Marriages: Hdt. 3.50, 6.35, 6.38.1, 6.128.2, and see R. Thomas, *Oral Tradition and Written Record in Classical Athens* (Cambridge 1989) 166–7. Tall poppies: Hdt. 5.92f-g and Arist. *Pol.* 1284a 26–33.

22. E.g. O. Murray, *Early Greece* (London 1993) 139.

23. On Cypselus see above n.3; Orthagorids: Arist. *Pol.* 1315b 14–16 and Nicolaus of Damascus *FGrH* 90 fr. 61.

24. Pausanias, *Description of Greece* 10.24.1, Hdt. 5.95.2.
25. See L. Gernet, 'Marriages of tyrants', in Gernet, L., *The Anthropology of Ancient Greece*, trans. J. Hamilton and B. Nagy (Baltimore 1981) 289–302.
26. Hdt. 1.59–64, 5.55–65, Arist. *Ath. Pol.* 14–19, Thuc. 6.53–9. See B.M. Lavelle, *The sorrow and the pity: a prolegomenon to a history of Athens under the Peisistratids, c.560–510 BC* (Stuttgart 1993) and R. Thomas, *Oral Tradition and Written Record in Classical Athens* (Cambridge 1989) ch. 5 on the traditions about the end of the tyranny.
27. Skolion: Fornara 39; statue of the tyrannicides: J. Boardman, *Greek Sculpture: the classical period* (London 1985) 24–5: Leipsydrion: Ar. *Lys.* 665–70; Pisistratids as good rulers: Arist. *Ath. Pol.* 16.1, 18.1.
28. See B.M. Lavelle, 'The compleat angler: observations on the rise of Peisistratos in Herodotus (1.59–64)', *CQ* 41 (1991) 317–24.
29. In general on the Pisistratid tyranny, see A. Andrewes, 'The Tyranny of Pisistratus', *CAH²* III 392–416 and D.M. Lewis, 'The Tyranny of the Pisistratidai', *CAH²* IV 287–302. Building projects: see J.S. Boersma, *Athenian Building Policy from 561–560 to 404–403 BC* (Groningen 1970); *archonships*: M-L 6 (= Fornara 23C), roads: [Plato] *Hipparchos* 228c; Homeric redaction: Cic. *De Orat.* 3.137.
30. Aeaces and Syloson: Hdt. 3.139–149, 6.13 and 25; see G. Shipley, *A History of Samos* (Oxford 1984) chs 4 and 6, and J. P. Barron, 'The sixth-century tyranny at Samos', *CQ* 14 (1964), 210–49.
31. On the Persian empire, see L. Allen, *The Persian Empire* (Chicago 2005), M. Austin, 'Greek tyrants and the Persians, 546–479 BC', *CQ* 40 (1990) 289–306; Themistocles: Thuc. 1.135–8, Plut. *Them.* 29.7; coins: C. Howgego, *Ancient History From Coins* (London 1995) no. 31 and p.64; see H.A. Cahn and D. Gerin, 'Themistocles at Magnesia', *Num. Chron.* 148 (1988) 13–20.
32. Hippias: Hdt. 5.63–5, 90–1; Ambracia: Arist. *Pol.* 1304a 31–3; Sicyon: P. Ryland 18, and see A. Griffin, *Sikyon* (Oxford 1982) 45–7; A. Andrewes, *The Greek Tyrants* (London 1956) p. 127.
33. Dedications: Diod. 11.26.7, Fornara 54 and see S. Harrell, 'King or private citizen: fifth-century Sicilian tyrants at Olympia and Delphi', *Mnemosyne* 55 (2002) 439–64.
34. Kingship: S.I. Oost, 'The tyrant kings of Syracuse', *Class. Phil.* 71 (1976) 224–36.
35. On the Deinomenids, see M.I. Finley, *Ancient Sicily* (London 1979) ch. 4; marriages: Diod. 11.48.5, Schol. Pind. *Ol.* ii, Finley p.47; Hieron

succeeds: Diod. 11.38.7; Aeschylus: *Life of Aeschylus* 4.15, in M.R. Lefkowitz, *Lives of the Greek Poets* (London 1981); spies: Arist. *Pol.* 1313a 12–14 and F.S. Russell, *Information Gathering in Classical Greece* (Ann Arbor 1999) 106–14; Thrasyboulus: Diod. 11.66.4.

36. Rhegium: Hdt. 6.23; Cumae: Dion. Hal. 6.21.3; Etruria: Dion. Hal. 5.21.3, Livy 2.9.1; Roman kings: see F. Glinister, 'Kingship and tyranny in archaic Rome', in S. Lewis (ed.), *Ancient Tyranny* (Edinburgh 2006) and T.J. Cornell, *The Beginnings of Rome: Rome and Italy from the Bronze Age to the Punic Wars* (London 1995) 143–50.

37. Thrasydaeus: Diod. 11.53; Thrasyboulus: Diod. 11.67.5–68.4; sons of Anaxilas: Diod. 11.76.5. *Politeia*: Ar. *Pol.* 1304a 27–9.

38. Hdt. 6.123; *archon* lists: M-L 6 (= Fornara 23); history of the Alcmaeonids: Hdt. 6.125–131. See R. Thomas, *Oral Tradition and Written Record in Classical Athens* (Cambridge 1989) ch. 5.

39. Miltiades prosecuted: Hdt. 6.104; 'friends of the tyrants': Arist. *Ath Pol.* 22.4; regulations for Erythrae: M-L 40 (= Fornara 71).

40. See R. Osborne, and L. Mitchell, 'Tyrannical oligarchs at Athens', in S. Lewis (ed.), *Ancient Tyranny* (Edinburgh 2006) 178–87 and J.F. McGlew, *Tyranny and Political Culture in Ancient Greece* (Ithaca and London 1993) ch. 6; on laws, I. Arnaoutoglou, *Ancient Greek Law: a sourcebook* (London and New York 1998) no. 64 and M. Ostwald, 'The Athenian legislation against tyranny and subversion', *TAPA* 86 (1955) 103–28.

41. Philoxenus: Diod. 15.6.2–5; other tales: Cic. *Tusc. Disp.* 5.57–63. See B. Caven, *Dionysius I, Warlord of Syracuse* (1990) and D.M. Lewis, 'Sicily, 413–368 BC', *CAH*² VI, 120–155.

42. Decision of the assembly: Diod. 14.45; family: Diod. 14.62, 63, 102, 109.2, Xen. *Hell.* 5.1.26, Plut. *Dion* 4.1–2, 5.8. Sons: R-O 33.

43. Sparta intervenes: Diod. 14.10.2–4 and 14.70; ships sent to aid Sparta: Xen. *Hell.* 6.2.33, 7.1.20, 28; inscriptions from Athens: R-O 10 (393), R-O 33 (369), R-O 34 (368).

44. Omens: Schol. Aesch. 2.10, Val. Max. 1.7.6, Philistus *FGrHist* 556 fr. 58 (= Gel. 12.46), Cic. *De Div.* 1.73, and see S. Lewis, 'The tyrant's myth', in C.J. Smith and J. Serrati (eds), *Sicily from Aeneas to Augustus* (Edinburgh 2000) 97–106; marriages: Diod. 14.44.6–8 and L. Gernet, 'Marriages of tyrants', in Gernet, *The Anthropology of Ancient Greece*, trans. J. Hamilton and B. Nagy (Baltimore 1981) 289–302; family structure: Caven 243.

45. See J.A.O. Larson, *Greek Federal States: their institutions and history* (Oxford 1968) 12–26 and S. Sprawski, *Jason of Pherae: a study on the history of Thessaly in the years 431–370 BC* (1999).

46. See S. Sprawski, 'Were Lycophron and Jason tyrants of Pherai?', in C.J. Tuplin (ed.), *Xenophon and His World. Papers from a conference held in Liverpool in July 1999* (*Historia* Einzelschriften 172) (Stuttgart 2004) 437–52.

47. See S. Sprawski, 'Alexander of Pherae: infelix tyrant', in S. Lewis (ed.), *Ancient Tyranny* (Edinburgh 2006) 135–147.

48. See S. Hornblower, *Mausolus* (Oxford 1982) and S. Ruzicka, *Politics of a Persian dynasty: the Hecatomnids in the fourth century B.C.* (Norman, OK 1992).

49. Inscription: Hornblower, *Mausolus* pp.70–71, Arist. *Oik.* 2.1348a 4; comedy: Athenaeus *Deipn.* 472e-f. See Ruzika, *Politics of a Persian Dynasty* 43–4. On kingship, Hornblower, *Mausolus* 59–62.

50. M-L 7 (= Fornara 24). See M. Trundle, *Greek Mercenaries: from the late archaic period to Alexander* (London 2004).

51. On Pittacus, see above pp. 20–1; dedications of Gelon and Hieron: M-L 28 and 29 (= Fornara 54 and 64).

52. Demosthenes, *Third Philippic*; Diodorus 15.76.1; Aeschines 3 (*Against Ctesiphon*) 85–91, 103; see P.A. Brunt, 'Euboia in the time of Philip II', *CQ* 19 (1969) 245–65 and G.L. Cawkwell, 'Euboia in the late 340s', *Phoenix* 32 (1978) 42–67.

53. R-O 79, Schwenk no. 6. See M. Ostwald, 'The Athenian legislation against tyranny and subversion', *TAPA* 86 (1955) 103–28.

54. Thebes: Xen. *Hell.* 5.2.25–36, 5.4.1–13; Plut. *Pelopidas* 5–13; Thirty Tyrants: Xen. *Hell.* 2.3–4; Lysias 12 (*Against Eratosthenes*) and P. Krentz, *The Thirty at Athens* (Ithaca and London 1982); Epaminondas: Plut. *Pel.* 25 and J. Buckler, *The Theban Hegemony 371–362 BC* (Cambridge, MA and London 1980) ch. 6.

55. See W.R. Connor, 'Tyrannis *polis*', in J.H. D'Arms and J.W. Eadie (eds), *Ancient and Modern: essays in honour of G.F. Else* (Ann Arbor 1977) 95–109.

56. See M. Schofield, *Saving the City: philosopher-kings and other classical paradigms* (1999), ch.2 (The disappearing philosopher-king).

57. See G.R. Morrow, *Plato's Epistles* (Indianapolis 1962), L. Edelstein, *Plato's Seventh Letter* (Leiden 1966), N. Gulley, 'The authenticity of Plato's Epistles', *Pseudepigrapha I* (Geneva 1972) ch. 5.

58. *Aisymneteia* is included as a form of monarchy at *Pol.* 1285a 29-b3, and of tyranny at 1295a1–16.
59. P. Green, 'Politics, philosophy and propaganda: Hermias of Atarneus and his friendship with Aristotle', in W. Heckel and L.A. Tritle, *Crossroads of History: the age of Alexander* (Claremont 2003) 29–46.
60. Plut. *Demetrius* 10; Pausanias *Description of Greece* 1.25.6; see W.W. Fortenbaugh and E. Schütrumpf, *Demetrius of Phalerum: text, translation and discussion* (New Brunswick and London 2000).
61. V.J. Gray, 'Xenophon and Isocrates' in C. Rowe and M. Schofield (eds), *The Cambridge History of Greek and Roman Political Thought* (Cambridge 2000) ch.7.
62. Our accounts of Clearchus' reign are to be found in Justin *Epitome* 16.4.1–5.18 and the fragmentary history of Memnon; see S.M. Burstein, *Outpost of Hellenism: the emergence of Heraclea on the Black Sea* (Berkeley 1976) 3–4.
63. Burstein, *Outpost of Hellenism* 61.
64. Burstein, *Outpost of Hellenism* ch. 5.
65. See J. Ma, 'Kings', in A. Erskine (ed.), *A Companion to the Hellenistic World* (Oxford 2003) 177–195, D.E. Hahm, 'Kings and constitutions', in C. Rowe and M. Schofield (eds), *The Cambridge History of Greek and Roman Political Thought* (Cambridge 2000) ch. 23, and E.S. Gruen, 'Hellenistic Kingship: puzzles, problems and possibilities', in P. Bilde *et al.* (eds), *Aspects of Hellenistic Kingship* (Studies in Hellenistic Civilization VII) (Aarhus 1996) 116–25.
66. E.g. H. Berve, *Die Tyrannis bei den Griechen* I (Munich 1967) 259–60, K.F. Stroheker, *Dionysios I: Gestalt und Geschichte des Tyrannen von Syrakus* (Wiesbaden 1969) 183.
67. Diod. 19.1.7 (rule of Libya); Italian campaigns: Diod. 21.4, 8, Justin 23.1–2; marriages: Lanassa, Plut. *Pyrrh.* 9.1; Theoxene, Justin 23.2.6; purges: Diod. 20.63 and 72. See K. Meister, 'Agathocles', *CAH²* VII.1 384–411.
68. B.V. Head, *Historia numorum. A Manual of Greek Numismatics* (Oxford 1911) 181–2 and E. Zambon, 'From Agathocles to Hieron II: the birth and development of *basileia* in Hellenistic Sicily', in S. Lewis (ed.), *Ancient Tyranny* (Edinburgh 2006) 77–92.
69. P. Oxy XXIV.2933: Diod. 21.16.3. 20.63.1, 21.16.2. See S. Lewis, 'Tyranny and kingship in Syracuse', *Electrum* (11) 2006 45–59.
70. Head, *Historia numorum* 182 and R. Ross Holloway, 'Eagle and fulmen on the coins of Syracuse', *RBN* 108 (1962) 5–28.
71. Dionysius: *IG* ii² 18, 103, 105 and 523; Diog. Laert. 2.66, Cic. *Tusc.*

5.58, 61; S.I. Oost, S.I., 'The tyrant kings of Syracuse', *Class. Phil.* 71 (1976) 224–236, esp. 236. Royal gate: Diod. 15.74.5.

72. Justin 16.5.9–10, Plut. *Mor.* 338B; Memnon *FGrH* 434 F1.1; S.M. Burstein, *Outpost of Hellenism: the emergence of Heraclea on the Black Sea* (Berkeley 1974) 61.

73. Hicetas: Diod. 22.7.2–3, 6, Justin 24.4.1; Thoenon and Sosistratos: Plut. *Pyrrh.* 23, Dion. Hal. 20.8; Pyrrhus: Plut. *Pyrrh.* 23.3–4, Dion. Hal. 20.8.1. See Zambon, 'From Agathocles to Hieron II' (above n.2). For Hieron, see below.

74. On Royal Friends, see G. Shipley, *The Greek World after Alexander 323–30 BC* (London 2000) 76–7 and F. W. Walbank, *The Hellenistic World* (London 1981) 75–7.

75. Pericles: Thuc.2.65; Epaminondas: Plut. *Pelop.* 24–5, 27, 29.

76. Polyb. 1.16, Livy 22.37; lavish life: Polyb. 7.8; Archimedes' mirrors: Cass. Dio 15 (= Zonaras 9.4, Tzetzes *Chil.* 2.109–128). On Hieron, see M.I. Finley, *Ancient Sicily* (London 1979) ch. 9.

77. Head, *Historia numorum* 183–5, G.K. Jenkins, *Ancient Greek Coins* (London and New York 1972) nos. 596–7, 603–4, 636–7; see Lewis, 'Tyranny and kingship in Syracuse (above n. 70).

78. Deinomenid ancestry: Justin 23.4.4 (which also reproduces the story of Gelon's rescue by a wolf in childhood (Diod. 10.29)); names of children: Livy 23.30.11, 24.22.8, Polybius 7.8, Paus. 6.12.2–4. On the omens surrounding the birth and youth of the tyrants, S. Lewis, 'The tyrant's myth', in C.J. Smith and J. Serrati, (eds), *Sicily from Aeneas to Augustus* (Edinburgh 2000) 97–106.

79. I. Gildenhard, 'Reckoning with tyranny: Greek thoughts on Caesar in Cicero's *Letters to Atticus* in early 49', in S. Lewis (ed.), *Ancient Tyranny* (Edinburgh 2006) 197–209.

80. Diod. 19.9.1–6; B.M. Lavelle, *Fame, Money, and Power: the rise of Peisistratos and 'democratic' tyranny at Athens* (Ann Arbor 2005) 77, 90.

81. See J. Salmon, 'Lopping off the heads? Tyrants, politics and the *polis*', in L.G. Mitchell and P.J. Rhodes (eds), *The Development of the Polis in Archaic Greece* (London 1997) 60–73; Dion. Hal. 5.70; Cass. Dio 54.1.3–4, Suet. *Aug.* 52.

82. See above chapters 3 and 4. Sicily in the 460s, when according to Diodorus (11.53, 68) most states threw out their tyrants, is perhaps an interesting exception.

83. Dionysius: Diod. 14.45, and see also Livy 24.22 for the assembly under Hieron.

FURTHER READING

The reading below is organised by theme or individual and is intended
to be introductory; a few works in European languages are included,
but most are in English. English-speaking bibliography on tyranny has
long been dominated by Andrewes' *The Greek Tyrants* (London 1956),
which examines archaic tyranny in detail as far as the Deinomenids,
with a final chapter on the later tyrants. Andrewes' book is the *locus
classicus* of the 'age of tyranny' theory, suggesting that tyranny was a
stage through which the *polis* had to pass on its way to political maturity,
but is now rather dated. Mossé's *La tyrannie dans la Grèce antique* (Paris
1969) takes a longer perspective, covering archaic and classical tyranny
down to the rule of Nabis in Sparta. She emphasises the role of the
tyrant as representative of the *demos*, seeing economic conditions as the
most significant factor in tyrannical rule. A much more thoroughgoing
study is Berve's *Die Tyrannis bei den Griechen* (Munich 1967), which
offers a discussion and complete collection of ancient evidence for every
known or potential tyrant, from the archaic to the hellenistic period.
Berve makes a sharp division between early and late tyranny, seeing the
latter as distinct in character, but includes a very interesting section
on fifth-century tyrannies. More modern studies of tyranny in English
have been few: Morgan's collection *Popular Tyranny* (Austin, TX 2003),
despite its title, is focused entirely on Athens, and most other studies
(such as McGlew's thought-provoking *Tyranny and Political Culture in
Archaic Greece* (Ithaca 1993)) have confined themselves to consideration
of archaic tyrannies. There has been a particular interest in Pisistratid
Athens and the 'end of tyranny', implicitly following a model in which
an 'age of tyranny' facilitates the emergence of democracy. Brock and
Hodkinson's *Alternatives to Athens* (Oxford 2000) made a welcome break
with this model, investigating the variety of political systems used in
classical Greece. My own collection *Ancient Tyranny* (Edinburgh 2006),

which originated in a conference held in 2003 to look at the persistence of tyranny in Greek history, focuses on fifth- and fourth-century tyrannies.

Introductory

C. Mossé, *La tyrannie dans la Grèce antique* (Paris 1969).

H. Berve, *Die Tyrannis bei den Griechen* (2 vols, Munich 1967).

S. Lewis (ed.), *Ancient Tyranny* (Edinburgh 2006).

A. Andrewes, *The Greek Tyrants* (London 1956).

R. Brock and S. Hodkinson (eds), *Alternatives to Athens: varieties of political organization and community in ancient Greece* (Oxford 2000).

K.A. Morgan (ed.), *Popular Tyranny: sovereignty and its discontents* (Austin, TX 2003).

Introductions to political theory

R. Balot, *Greek Political Thought* (Oxford 2006).

C. Rowe and M. Schofield (eds), *The Cambridge History of Greek and Roman Political Thought* (Cambridge 2000).

D. Keyt and F. Miller, 'Ancient Greek Political Thought', in G.F. Gaus and C. Kukathas (eds), *A Handbook of Political Theory* (London 2004) 303–19.

R. Brock and S. Hodkinson, 'Introduction: alternatives to the democratic polis', in Brock and Hodkinson (eds), *Alternatives to Athens: varieties of political organization and community in ancient Greece* (Oxford 2000) 1–31.

M. Ostwald, *Oligarchia: the development of a constitutional form in ancient Greece* (*Historia* Einzelschriften 144) (Stuttgart 2000).

J.L. O'Neill, *The Origins and Development of Ancient Greek Democracy* (1995).

Development of ideas about tyranny

V. Parker, '*Tyrannos*: the semantics of a political concept from Archilochus to Aristotle', *Hermes* 126 (1998) 145–172.

R. Osborne, 'Changing the discourse', in K. Morgan (ed.), *Popular Tyranny* (Austin, TX 2003) 251–72.

J.L. O'Neill, 'The semantic usage of *tyrannos* and related words', *Antichthon*
20 (1986) 26–40.

C. Dewald, 'Form and content: the question of tyranny in Herodotus', in
K. Morgan (ed.), *Popular Tyranny* (Austin, TX 2003) 25–58.

S. Morris, 'Imaginary kings: alternatives to monarchy in early Greece', in
K. Morgan (ed.), *Popular Tyranny* (Austin, TX 2003) 1–24.

L.G. Mitchell, 'Tyrannical oligarchs at Athens', in S. Lewis (ed.), *Ancient
Tyranny* (Edinburgh 2006) 178–87.

C. B. R. Pelling, 'Speech and action: Herodotus' debate on the constitutions', *PCPS* 48 (2002) 123–58.

C. Tuplin, 'Imperial tyranny', in P.A. Catledge and F.D. Harvey (eds), *CRUX:
essays presented to G.E.M. de Ste. Croix on his 75th birthday* (London 1985)
348–75.

Chapter 1: Archaic tyrants
Introductory

J. McGlew, *Tyranny and Political Culture in Archaic Greece* (Ithaca 1993).

G.L. Cawkwell, 'Early Greek tyranny and the People', *CQ* 45 (1995)
73–86.

D. Ogden, *The Crooked Kings of Ancient Greece* (London 1996).

R. Drews, *Basileus: evidence for kingship in Geometric Greece* (London and
New Haven 1983).

P. Carlier, *La Royauté en Grèce avant Alexandre* (Strasbourg 1984).

Corinth

J.B.Salmon, *Wealthy Corinth* (Oxford 1984).

V.J. Gray, 'Herodotus and images of tyranny: the tyrants of Corinth' *AJPh*
117.3 (1996) 361–89.

S. Oost, 'Cypselus the Bacchiad', *Class. Phil.* 67 (1972), 10–30.

Mytilene

D. L. Page, *Sappho and Alcaeus* (Oxford 1979), 149–243.

R. Osborne, *Greece in the Making* (London and New York 2002), 190–7.

Sicyon

A. Griffin, *Sikyon* (Oxford 1982).

N. Hammond, 'The family of Orthagoras', *CQ* 6 (1956), 45–53.

Argos

T. Kelly, *A History of Argos* (Minneapolis 1976) ch. 7.

Chapter 2: The end of tyranny?
Athens

A. Andrewes, 'The tyranny of Pisistratus', *CAH²* III.3 392–416.

D.M. Lewis, 'The tyranny of the Pisistratidai', *CAH²* IV 287–302.

B.M. Lavelle, *The Sorrow and the Pity: a prolegomenon to a history of Athens under the Pisistratids, c.560–510 BC* (*Historia* Einzenschriften 80) (Stuttgart 1993).

B.M. Lavelle, *Fame, Money, and Power: the rise of Peisistratos and 'democratic' tyranny at Athens* (Ann Arbor 2005).

H. Sancisi-Weerdenburg, *Peisistratos and the Tyranny* (Amsterdam 2000).

J. S. Ruebel, 'The tyrannies of Peisistratos', *GRBS* 14 (1973) 125–36.

Samos

J. P. Barron, 'The sixth-century tyranny at Samos', *CQ* 14 (1964), 210–49.

G. Shipley, *A History of Samos, 800–188 BC* (Oxford 1984).

Ionia

M. Austin, 'Greek tyrants and the Persians 546–479 BC', *CQ* 40 (1990) 289–306.

R.J. Seager and C. Tuplin, 'The freedom of the Greeks of Asia', *JHS* 100 (1980) 141–57.

R. V. Munson, 'Artemisia in Herodotus', *Class. Ant.* 7 (1988) 91–106.

Sicily and the West

M.I. Finley, *Ancient Sicily* (London 1979).

T.J. Dunbabin, *The Western Greeks: The history of Sicily and South Italy from the foundation of the Greek colonies to 480 BC* (Oxford 1948).

R. Ross Holloway, *The Archaeology of Ancient Sicily* (London 1991).

S.I. Oost, 'The tyrant kings of Syracuse', *Class. Phil.* 71 (1976) 224–36.

S. Berger, *Revolution and Society in Greek Sicily and Southern Italy* (*Historia* Einzelschriften 71) (Stuttgart 1992).

Chapter 3: Tyranny remade?

A very useful introduction to the fourth century can be found in L. Tritle (ed.), *The Greek World in the Fourth Century* BC (London 1997), which has a chapter on each region of the Aegean.

Sicily

D.M. Lewis, 'Sicily, 413–368 BC', *CAH²* VI, 120–155.

B. Caven, *Dionysius I, Warlord of Syracuse* (New Haven 1990).

K.F. Stroheker, *Dionysios I: Gestalt und Geschichte des Tyrannen von Syrakus* (Wiesbaden 1969).

L.J. Sanders, *Dionysius of Syracuse and Greek Tyranny* (London 1987).

A.G. Woodhead, 'The "Adriatic Empire" of Dionysius I', *Klio* 53 (1970) 503–12.

S. Lewis, 'The tyrant's myth', in C.J. Smith and J. Serrati (eds), *Sicily from Aeneas to Cicero* (Edinburgh 2000) 97–106.

L. Pearson, *The Greek Historians of the West: Timaeus and his Predecessors* (Atlanta 1987).

Thessaly

J.A.O. Larsen, *Greek Federal States: their institutions and history* (Oxford 1968) 12–26.

S. Sprawski, *Jason of Pherae: a study on the history of Thessaly in the years 431–370 BC* (Krakow 1999).

S. Sprawski, 'Were Lycophron and Jason tyrants of Pherae?', in C.J. Tuplin (ed.), *Xenophon and his World. Papers from a conference held in Liverpool in July 1999* (*Historia* Einzelschriften 172) (Stuttgart 2004) 437–52.

S. Sprawski, 'Alexander of Pherae: infelix tyrant', in S. Lewis (ed.), *Ancient Tyranny* (Edinburgh 2006) 135–147.

H.D. Westlake, *Thessaly in the Fourth Century* BC (Groningen 1969).

J. Mandel, 'Jason: the tyrant of Pherai ...The Image of the New Tyrant', *Rivista storica dell' antichita* 10 (1980) 47–77.

H.T. Wade-Gery, 'Jason of Pherai and Aleuas the Red', *JHS* 44 (1924) 55–64.

Caria

S. Hornblower, *Mausolus* (Oxford 1982).

S. Ruzicka, *Politics of a Persian dynasty: the Hecatomnids in the fourth century B.C.* (Norman, OK 1992).

R.M. Berthold, 'Fourth-century Rhodes', *Historia* 29 (1980) 32–49.

C. Scarre, '"A tomb to wonder at" (the Mausoleum at Halicarnassus)', *Archaeology* 46.5 (1993) 32–39.

D. Gera, *Warrior Women* (Leiden 1997).

Euphron

A. Griffin, *Sikyon* (Oxford 1982).

S. Lewis, 'Xenophon's account of Euphron of Sicyon', *JHS* 124 (2004) 65–74.

D. Whitehead, 'Euphron, tyrant of Sicyon', *Liverpool Classical Monthly* 5.8 (1980) 175–8.

J. Dillery, *Xenophon and the History of his Times* (London and New York 1995).

Euboea

P.A. Brunt, 'Euboia in the time of Philip II', *CQ* 19 (1969) 245–65.

G.L. Cawkwell, 'Euboia in the late 340s', *Phoenix* 32 (1978) 42–67.

N.G. Hammond, *Philip of Macedon* (London 1994) chs 10 and 12.

Laws against tyranny

M. Ostwald, 'The Athenian legislation against tyranny and subversion', *TAPA* 86 (1955) 103–28.

V. J. Rosivach, 'The tyrant in Athenian democracy', *QUCC* 30 (1988) 43–57.

C. Mossé, 'A propos de la loi d'Eucrates sur la tyrannie (337/6 av. J.-C.)', *Eirene* 8 (1970) 73–6.

Chapter 4: Philosophers and tyrants
General

V.J. Gray, 'Xenophon's *Hiero* and the meeting of the wise man and the tyrant in Greek literature' *CQ* 31 (1981) 321–34.

G.J.D. Aalders, 'The date and intention of Xenophon's *Hiero*', *Mnemosyne* 6 (1953) 208–215.

L. Strauss, *On Tyranny: an interpretation of Xenophon's* Hiero, (revised edition, ed. V. Gourevitch and M. S. Roth) (Chicago 2000).

J. McGlew, *Tyranny and Political Culture in Archaic Greece* (Ithaca 1993) 206–12.

Plato

H.D. Westlake, 'Dion and Timoleon', *CAH*² VI, 693–722.

P.A. Brunt, 'Plato's Academy and politics', in P.A. Brunt, *Studies in Greek History and Thought* (Oxford 1993), ch. 10.

F.L. Vatai, *Intellectuals in Politics in the Greek World* (London 1984).

M. Schofield, *Saving the City: philosopher-kings and other classical paradigms* (London and New York 1999).

G.C. Field, *Plato and His Contemporaries: a study in fourth-century life and thought* (London 1967).

H.D. Westlake, 'Dion: a study in liberation', in H.D. Westlake, *Essays on the Greek Historians and Greek History* (Manchester 1969), 251–64.

A.S. Riginos, *Platonica: the anecdotes concerning the life and writings of Plato* (Leiden 1976).

G.R. Morrow, *Plato's Cretan City* (Princeton 1960).

Aristotle

A. Lintott, 'Aristotle and the mixed constitution', in R. Brock and S. Hodkinson (eds), *Alternatives to Athens* (Oxford 2000) 152–66.

D. Keyt and F.D. Miller Jr, *A Companion to Aristotle's Politics* (Oxford 1991).

R.G. Mulgan, *Aristotle's Political Theory: an introduction* (Oxford 1977).

P.L.P. Simpson, *A Philosophical Commentary on the* Politics *of Aristotle* (Chapel Hill and London 1998)

J. Barnes *et al.* (eds), *Articles on Aristotle, vol. 2, Ethics and Politics* (London 1977).

M. Nichols, *Citizens and Statesmen: A Study of Aristotle's Politics* (Savage, MD 1992).

P. Green, 'Politics, philosophy and propaganda: Hermias of Atarnaeus and his friendship with Aristotle', in W. Heckel and L.A. Tritle (eds), *Crossroads of History: the age of Alexander* (Claremont, CA 2003) 29–46.

C. Habicht, *Athens from Alexander to Anthony* (Harvard 1999).

W.S. Ferguson, *Hellenistic Athens: an historical essay* (ed.² New York 1969).

W.W. Fortenbaugh and E. Schütrumpf, *Demetrius of Phalerum: text, translation and discussion* (New Brunswick 2000).

S. Dow and A.H. Travis, 'Demetrios of Phaleron and his lawgiving', *Historia* 12 (1943).

Isocrates

V.J. Gray, 'Xenophon and Isocrates' in C. Rowe and M. Schofield (eds), *The Cambridge History of Greek and Roman Political Thought* (Cambridge 2000) ch.7.

P. Lévèque, *Isocrate et son temps* (Paris 1963).

K.A. Morgan, 'The tyranny of the audience in Plato and Isocrates', in K.A. Morgan (ed.), *Popular Tyranny* (Austin, TX 2003) 181–213.

Heracleia

S.M. Burstein, *Outpost of Hellenism: the emergence of Heraclea on the Black Sea* (Berkeley 1976).

Chapter 5: Tyrants and kings
General

F.W. Walbank, *The Hellenistic World* (London 1981).

G. Shipley, *The Greek World after Alexander, 323–30 BC* (London and New York 2000).

A. Erskine (ed.), *A Companion to the Hellenistic World* (Oxford 2003).

Syracuse: from Agathocles to Hieron

M.I. Finley, *Ancient Sicily* (London 1979).

R. Ross Holloway, *The Archaeology of Ancient Sicily* (London 1991).

K. Meister, 'Agathocles', *CAH*² VII, 384–411.

E. Zambon, 'From Agathocles to Hieron II: the birth and development of *basileia* in Hellenistic Sicily', in S. Lewis (ed.), *Ancient Tyranny* (Edinburgh 2006) 77–92.

S. Lewis, 'Agathocles: tyranny and kingship in Syracuse', *Electrum* 11 (2006), 45–59.

S. Berger, *Revolution and Society in Greek Sicily and Southern Italy* (*Historia* Einzelschriften 71) (Stuttgart 1992) 49–53.

B.D. Hoyus, 'The rise of Hiero II: chronology and campaigns', *Antichthon* 19 (1985) 32–56.

A.M. Eckstein, 'Hieron II and Rome, 263–15', *Chiron* 10 (1980) 183–203.

Sicyon

A. Griffin, *Sikyon* (Oxford 1982).

F.W. Walbank, *Aratus of Sicyon* (Cambridge 1933).

F.W. Walbank, 'Macedonia and Greece', *CAH*² VII.1, 221–56.

J.A.O. Larsen, *Greek Federal States: their institutions and history* (Oxford 1968) 215–40.

INDEX